# Table of Contents

# Introduction

Cracking an interview is not like a cake walk anymore. The benchmarks have heightened with a giant leap and now the interviews are twice as challenging as they used to be. In order to crack an interview now, not only you need skill, but also the personality that convinces the interviewer that you are the right person for the job.

Gradually progressing through the book, one can easily understand the necessary qualities that the candidate should possess to clear an interview easily. This book has been complied after constant researches and references from the past through which one can look into the mistakes that the candidates have been making all along, while attending an interview.

There are many useful tips that could help you nail an interview with the highest score. Also, there are many illustrations of interview successes and blunders that people have been making in an interview.

Everything in this book is explained in detail in order to have no doubts at the end. The main goal behind publishing this book is to help the struggling candidates, who do not have proper guidance and hence, fail to understand the basic aspects of an interview.

I have also included the most common questions asked in an interview along with the tricky questions that leave you blank in front of the interviewers. Moreover, I have also included guides like how to dress for an interview and how to behave when you are attending one.

A person with this manual can easily understand what actually an interview is and will be able to attend any interview with better confidence level. Interviewing is not just about possessing skill and knowledge. One should understand that through the course of an interview, interviewers judge the mentality, determination, perseverance, behaviour and many more aspects that an ideal candidate needs to possess.

This book is perfect for every candidate, who is about to attend an interview. This book is an ultimate blueprint for a fresher to strengthen the basics. The book is also a 'step-by-step' guide for the candidates aspiring to change their jobs, who have not been successful in clearing the interviews so far. They would be able to identify the things they have been doing wrong in an interview. And yes, if you are the one who believes in planning and preparing well in advance, this book is a must have for you.

# CHAPTER 1

# Understanding What Interview Is

> *"An Interview is a procedure designed to obtain information from a person's oral response to oral inquiries."*
> *- Gary Dessler*

It is a common misconception that it is very easy to crack an interview if you have the knowledge. But most of the individuals ignore the basics and only focus on impressing the interviewers with the vast knowledge they posses. It is here that the candidates make simple and avoidable mistakes and are eliminated. In order to get the first job or career advancement, interview is one of the most important turning points in the life of a working professional. It is therefore very important to know the basics of an interview in order to understand the process of cracking one.

Around ninety percent of the candidates believe that the point of interview is to get the job. However, getting the job is the final point and there is still a whole process to go about. There are many references from where one can extract the definition of an interview, but the most common definition of an interview can be found on

Wikipedia, which defines interview as "A process in which a potential employee is evaluated by an employer for prospective employment in their company, organization, or a firm. During this process, the employer hopes to determine whether or not the applicant is suitable for the job."

The definition is actually given from an employer's point of view. However, there are still many aspects a candidate could extract from the given definition. The first and foremost point that a candidate has to understand is that an interview is a two way process, a process where an employer needs to understand the interviewee before giving her/him the suitable position in the firm. You need to know everything you can about the firm before you appear for the interview. Ask all the questions to the interviewer that cannot be found online or through valid references. Make sure that the job offered is legitimate. Ask all the questions to the interviewer that cannot be found and make sure that the job is very legitimate. The process of getting a job is also very similar to that of buying a flat. Before final registration, you make sure that the house is in a good condition and all the supplies you need like markets, school, bus stand, railway station, etc. are within a considerable range. Hurrying into the process might cause you a lot of problems later. Similarly in a job interview do not hurry and avoid nodding for every condition the interviewer puts forward. Your power to analyze everything and find the loopholes is very necessary here and you can only develop that ability by being a good observer.

So, what is an interview actually? When looked upon, the basic meaning of an interview is a gathering of two or more people to get a clear view of each other or knowing each other. There is a questionnaire conducted between those two persons, where one is the "Interviewer", who asks questions and the one answering the questions is called an "Interviewee".

*"Interview is a very systematic method by which a person enters deeply into the life of even a stranger and can bring out needed information and data for the research purpose".*
*- Dr. S. M. Amunuzzaman*

An interview can be of many types. There are more than 10 types of interviews. The most common type of interview is *"Personal Interview"*, but other types of interviews are also practiced widely. The concept in every interview is the same, just the method of conducting an interview changes.

The interview can have structured questions or a formal conversation, the basic aim of an interviewer is to assess the interviewee in every possible aspect. A candidate might not even know when the interview has begun and when it finished, but the interviewers have already got their answer. Some candidates take a longer time, while some come out in minutes; it is just the matter of expressing the right emotion at the right time.

*Once, there was a student, who came up to me asking, what is an interview? I simply replied "It is a questionnaire between interviewer(s) and interviewee, based on which the interviewer(s) concludes whether the interviewee is suitable for the applied post or not." With his keen eyes, I understood that he got the meaning and also concluded that I was the right person to ask the question. He came to me with his doubts and I helped him with them. He was a bright student, just lacked a bit of confidence, which after my guidance was not an issue anymore.*

Soon, one of his friend joined him and I was now helping two students prepare for an interview, which was about to be conducted in a month. The regular student was a quick learner even though he had less knowledge compared to his friend. On the other hand, the new student possessed a high IQ and was proud of it.

After a month of advice and hard work, both of them attended the interview and the student with less knowledge got the job, while the intelligent student was sent home. The reason was very simple, even though being knowledgeable, the new trainee was lacking at his fundamentals. He was smart and quick witted, but did not possess the right qualities like team work and socializing. The one that got the job was flexible and reacted according to the situation, which was a major plus point for him.

Similarly, I have come across many cases, where the knowledge was not the problem but the candidates were sent home because they just couldn't blend in with others. There was an occasion where I was an interviewer and I along with two more members was asked to select three out of twenty five candidates. We were supposed to judge the candidates on academics, sports, extracurricular activities and also behaviour wise.

Each interview lasted for fifteen to twenty minutes and on an average 20 of the 25 candidates did not have their preparations sorted. They were in a complete mess. They lacked in dressing style, confidence and behaviour too. I couldn't see the effort in them and had to reject them.

After that incident, I came to the conclusion that the candidates, who were rejected, did not have a proper guide to help them understand the situation. Their motivation was down and one could easily make out that they were not prepared for any sort of interview. Although their academic grades were considerably good, they lacked the basic knowledge of what an interview is.

## Different Types of Interview

There are many types of interviews, every interview being different from the other depending upon the method of interview. You can face any type of interview out of these different types. Even though there are different types of interview, the basic guidelines to prepare for an interview are quite similar. However, it is still very important to know and understand the different types of interviews to get the idea of the process through which you will be assessed.

## Informational Interview

The main objective of this interview can be defined in just one word, learning which is mostly conducted by a Career Counselor. You attend this interview to know more about a particular career option, employer or a particular job. Asking questions to the interviewing experts is also one extra way to understand the process deeper. Whatever knowledge you will gain here will help you critically grow your career and network.

These interviews are conducted by professionals in the counseling field, who first assess you and then based on your strong points suggest you to pursue the field you are good in.

## Telephonic Interview

This is also known as a screening interview method, because a telephonic interview is cost effective and can help screen candidates faster, generally from a geographically far away location. A telephonic interview generally lasts from 10 minutes to 30 minutes. This is more like an open book exam, where it is recommended to keep handy your resume, job description, reference list, prepared answers to tricky question and also details about the company. Since, the interviewers cannot see your body language, you have an advantage. However, you need to give polished answers without taking too many pauses between two sentences. It is very important to stay positive throughout the interview and always speak with an energetic tone.

## Individual or Personal Interview

Most commonly known as a personal interview, this is one of the most practiced interviews till date. I am sure you might have already experienced a few; it is just a face to face conversation between the interviewer and the interviewee. A personal interview generally can be 10 to 40 minutes, in which you need to answer almost all questions in a confident and a perfect tone. If the length of the interview is longer than 40 minutes, answer the questions in depth, using specific examples to support your facts and skills.

## Panel or Committee Interview

This is also a type of a personal interview; the only difference is that there is more than one hiring manager or decision maker. This can be a very challenging experience if you are not well prepared and can leave a strong impression at the back of your head. Be sure to maintain your body language well and maintain constant eye contact with every one, no matter who asked the question. You need to create a lasting image in all the eyes, because there are multiple considerations involved in this.

## Task Oriented Interview

This can be more like writing an exam or maybe attending a practical. You will be asked to apply your skills in solving problems and demonstrate your way of thinking. A company can ask you to write a small test to prove your intelligence or this can also be used as a screening method. For example, in SSB interview, which is one of the toughest interviews in India, and is opted to interview candidates who aspire to join Indian Army as officers, the candidates are asked to write a small screening test to qualify for the rest of the interview.

## MBA Interview

This type of an interview is specially conducted for students aspiring to complete their MBA degree. This is conducted only for the students, who clear specific exams conducted by the universities in India. Most of the times, it involves a personal interview and a group discussion.

## Visa Interview

Visa interviews are conducted for students, tourists, businessman or any other professionals who desire to travel abroad. These interviews are commonly conducted by Visa Officers. This interview is conducted to find the objective of travelling abroad. Since every country has its own policies to grant entry into its country and the Visa Interview for that country is based on these policies.

## Process of an Interview

Yes, this is true. There is actually a logical process for an interview. It may not be necessary that all the interviews follow the same process; I have prepared the most common process for an interview that is usually followed. Knowing how the interview will go about, you will be able to anticipate the interviewer's next move and perform with greater confidence.

*Entering the interview room* - Do not arrive too early for the interview. You are not there to clean the room and set the tables, arrive no more than 10 to 15 minutes early. Check yourself for the final time and see if everything is in its place. It is true that the interview is started as soon as you walk in through the door. Everything you do and everything you say will be evaluated once you enter the room, more like being on a stage. Be sure to treat everyone with respect, not only the hiring managers, but also the receptionist and even the peon, you never know who is going to talk about your behaviour outside the room. Be completely relaxed and do not show that you are nervous in any manner.

*Greeting*- As soon as you enter the room, you have to greet your hiring managers. Make sure you stand up straight, smile and look no where other than their eyes. Shake their hands if the opportunity presents and introduce yourself confidently. First impression and the body language are extremely important as you can decide the fate of the interview at this point. You can feel as if it is the first day at your job, which will give you enough positive vibes and reduce your anxiety.

*Getting comfortable* - Obviously, the interviewer understands that you are a bit nervous and will make you feel comfortable by starting the conversation with simple topic such as weather, health, parking etc. Absolutely make sure to avoid any controversial matters like religion or politics, you are not there to discuss the next step Prime Minister has to take. Observe everything inside the room, especially any picture or portraits on the wall that decorate the office. Make positive comments about the pictures and try to connect to them so that it could be easier to break the ice. Try to get the interviewer to like you, this display your social skills and the ability to blend in the crowd.

*Interview Expectations–* The interviewer may start with going through your resume and ask you some basic questions. Try to understand how lengthy the interview can be so you can adjust your answers accordingly. Do not interrupt the hiring manager while he is speaking, if you have any questions, save them for the end. Always be ready to respond sincerely to any question that will be asked from here on.

*General Interview Discussion–* After the interviewer has asked all the simple questions, slowly the interview will turn towards relevant subjects that they are actually interested in, more like your education, experience, skills and interests. It is important that you reply to each and every question with confidence and without any mistake, talk proudly about your achievements and give specific examples to prove your answer. Make sure you listen to the question properly, analyze the question from all angles and then give an optimistic answer.

*Further Inspection–* Now the interviewer will test your skills and qualifications that are essential for the job. Here, you will need to provide a few examples from your past that convinces the interviewer of your abilities. The interviewer will try to analyze you in every possible way by giving you situations that are very stressful, wrong or contradicting to your ideas, reply them with a cool head to let the interviewer know that you can handle it all. You can expect questions starting from: How? Why? What?

*Asking Questions–* As mentioned earlier, an interview is a two way process and you need to ask the questions that are bothering you. Ask intelligent and relevant questions that will clarify all your doubts about the job and the organization. Do not try to outsmart the interviewer with questions that she or he cannot answer, it may give out some negative signals. Try to demonstrate your enthusiasm for the job and leave the hiring manager with a positive impression.

*Closing*- By this time you will be getting cues from the interviewer that it is the time to wrap up. Do not miss these final minutes by just saying a "thank-you" and leaving. Be sure to say something convincing as for the last impression. Talk about your interest in this job and why you are serious getting the position. Also ask them about the next step that should be taken, also enquire when will you hear from them again and request a business card. Remember to thank them for spending time interviewing you and firmly shake hands while smiling and maintain the eye contact as you part ways. Also leave a warm regards for anyone you meet at the office.

*Follow up*- Always make sure to follow up with a thank-you letter or a note immediately. If you did not receive any notice by the time they told you would, call them once to check if you are still being considered for the job.

You need to understand the basics first before you start preparing for an interview. Understand different types and stages of an interview and plan your actions accordingly. Do not be lazy and think that everything can be managed in the last minute. Your preparation determines your desire to get the job. The harder you prepare the better chances you have in landing the job. Read on to know the steps you need to take to prepare for an interview.

# CHAPTER 2

# Steps To Prepare For an Interview

It is such a happy moment, when an invitation to an interview for a job you applied is received. You spend the rest of the day in a happy mood and imagine the scenarios that will take place in your life after getting the job. It is a human tendency to dream about all the things desired in life. But are you putting any effort to achieve that dream? Are you really preparing for an interview? You wanted certain marks in your tenth and exams after that, so you worked very hard because you knew it is important. Similarly, interview has the potential to make or break your career.

You are not the only one invited for the interview; there are other candidates about whom you know nothing. You never know if there is someone with greater potential and skills to bag that job instead of you. In order to win from your competitors and in fact all the candidates battling for the same position you need to do things differently.

It is always better to proceed in a systematic order. Jumping from one topic to other without any aim will leave you with nothing but confusion. You need to take it slow and steady and then gradually increase the time and effort you are putting into it. Just like the school students are advised to have a time table stuck on their board or somewhere near the study table, make a time table for yourself and do the same.

In order to clear any interview, follow the steps below and your preparation will be taken care of.

## Prepare a Professional Resume

*It is important to know that "69% of the candidates are rejected because they do not have a good resume."*

It is righteously said that the first impression is the last impression. Your resume reaches the interviewers before they see you personally. They know a lot about you written in the resume and has already created a mental image of you. The shape and contents of your resume gives them your image in their head.

An ideal resume is well organized, without any grammatical errors. The paper is out of spelling mistakes and also contains business communication language. Most of the candidates are selected because they have successfully impressed the HR managers with their resumes.

It is important to know that "69% of the candidates are rejected because they do not have a good resume."

But to understand how to write a good resume, it is important to understand what is a resume first. A resume is a document in which you include all your basic information with your skills and experience in order to give a brief summary about why are you suitable for the job. It sounds very simple to write a resume, but as mentioned earlier, factually, 69% of the candidates are rejected because they do not have a good resume.

The next question that needs to be asked is why do you need a resume? Unless and until you have a great link in the company you are applying, which can guarantee a job, you need a resume. The main motive of the resume is to let the HR manager know that you are qualified for the job and you have the potential to learn more. Remember, the resume you prepare is your first impression; it needs to be the best.

Many interviewees don't know how to write a good resume and what all should be included to make it more appealing. Just imagine yourself being an interviewer and looking for a potential candidate to fill up the employee gap in your firm. You post a job listing and include the essential qualifications and skills for the job. You will receive numerous candidates applying for the job and each one will have a different resume. You will see resumes piling up and eventually adding up to the collection. Out of these many resumes, you only need one potential candidate. You spend a lot of time going through all the resumes and throwing the irrelevant ones in the trash. There are many resumes with spelling and grammar mistakes, most of them do not even qualify for the job, many who qualify have no experience and many have completely irrelevant skills that are not needed for the job. Out of all the trash, you are looking for one resume which is good enough to attend the next stage and then you find one, a good neat resume with everything written in a proper manner. You mark that one and call that particular candidate for the interview. Then again you go back to your hunt.

Coming back to reality, imagine the situation of an interviewer, with so much of frustration he or she will just reject the resume which is not written properly or which has mistakes. As a job seeker, it is important for you to submit a resume which is eye catching. You need to prepare a proper layout of the resume you are preparing. Write your resume in rough and then correct it for mistakes until you think that it cannot be corrected more. Match your skills that are relevant to the job description and include only those. Do not worry if your resume is small and has not many words included. Instead of including words, always focus on including "keywords" that are relevant to the post that you are applying for. Many of the hiring companies now use a new technology called "Applicant Tracking System". This is nothing but simple software that scans your resume for relevant keywords and gives the score for your resume. If your score meets the cut-off score, you are invited for the job. Therefore, it is not at all necessary that you have to prepare a long resume, which has skills that are completely irrelevant to the job.

The basic template of your resume can be as follows.

# CANDIDATES NAME
(Basic Info with contact details)

(Cover Letter) Write something about you and why you are seeking for this job. Explain in brief about how good you are for this job. (The cover letter should not go more that 60 to 80 words)

_______________________________________________

_______________________________________________

_______________________________________________

## EDUCATION
(Include your education qualifications and where did you achieve them from)

_______________________________________________

_______________________________________________

## SKILLS
(Include only the relevant skills for the job and certifications, if any)

_______________________________________________

_______________________________________________

## EXPERIENCE
(If you have worked in any previous company, include how many years have you worked in that profession? What were your key result areas and achievements? Certificates, courses that you have completed, sports or any other activity certificate(s))

_______________________________________________

_______________________________________________

_______________________________________________

_______________________________________________

## EXTRA CURRICULAR
(Write about your other achievements and community involvement)

_______________________________________________

_______________________________________________

_______________________________________________

_______________________________________________

_______________________________________________

The above given template is just an example and anyone can follow any format that one finds appropriate. There is no specific format recommended for resume, however, the only condition is that it should contain only the relevant details and no false data. I have compiled a few tips that can help you to create a good resume.

- Apart from avoiding grammatical mistakes, make sure you follow a simple yet effective format.
- Mention your career objective at the start and ensure that it attracts the HR managers' attention.
- Make sure your personal credentials are correct and updated.
- If you are a fresher, mention it in your resume. It gives a scope of learning and it is way better than telling them directly.
- If you are changing your job, mention that too. Be precise about your current condition.
- If in case, you have an employment gap, mention that too, but also prepare a valid and a convincing reason for the same.
- Make sure that you use only one type of font in your entire resume.
- Your resume should not be of more than three pages.

It is important to know where you stand. Match your skills and qualifications you have with the ones mentioned in the job description. Attending an interview while ignoring the fact that you actually don't qualify for the job will be too much of a setback. An interviewer averagely takes around five to seven seconds to review the candidate's resume. When you apply for a job in a large corporate, they will filter candidates based on the resume. If it is not complete, appealing and relevant to the post you are applying for, you will lose the opportunity to be invited for the interview.

## Make a List of Strengths with Examples

During an interview, it is asked "What are your strengths?" This is one of the most common question asked and one of the toughest one too. Many candidates have no idea about how to actually answer this question. When asked about their strengths, they talk about their heroic activities they displayed once upon a time or maybe how good they can drive a motorbike. And when it comes to weaknesses, they completely go off the record, telling about the difficulty in attending morning classes in college or their fear against spider or any other insects or some say, "I am short tempered."

This sounds absolutely irrelevant to the ears of HR manager. They are not interviewing you to know your heroic deeds on motorbike or your fear of insects. They are only interested in knowing if you are good enough for the job and the company. If they want to know anything other than your job qualities, they will ask you personally. So how actually can you answer this question?

As mentioned before, many candidates cannot talk about their strengths well; therefore you have an opportunity to stand out of the crowd if you answer this question in a very compelling and authentic way. (Those who cannot speak well and have difficulty expressing their answers; they can always join the "Business English Course". Considering the high demand, I conduct this course very often to train the professionals, so that they can express well using Business English Phrases.) To begin with, your answer has to convince the HR manager for the following

- Your answer should be relevant to the company's needs
- You can easily meet the job requirements
- There is no need to look for someone else because you are perfect for the job
- You have skills and qualities that allow you to handle critical situations
- Your strengths can benefit the entire company

In order to make a list of your strengths and weaknesses you need to spend some time thinking and self evaluating. Include at least 10 strengths and also include examples, facts, incidents and convincing stories with numbers if possible that could prove them. In your list of strengths, you can include your:

- Confidence
- Experience
- Social compatibility
- Team work
- Education and training
- Communication skills
- Relevant talents like writing proposals and corrections

- Leadership qualities
- Influencing others
- Positive attitude

Narrow your list down to five minimum strengths about which you are comfortable talking. You can go more than five if you want to, but the chances are that you may not be asked to talk about all of them. Also, develop a story which proves them relevant; do not forget to check the loopholes in developing the story. Many times the HR manager can ask you a question regarding the story and you should be able to answer them confidently.

Below are mentioned a few example answers by which you can clearly demonstrate your strengths.

### For a fresher

*"Sir, my greatest strength has to be the ability to analyze and learn things quickly. For example, I was representing my college in an Inter College Cultural Fest and I was introduced to the team just the day before the competition. I was able to learn the facts and figures in just one day and presented them in a great manner. I was greatly praised by my teammates, teachers and seniors for this achievement."*

*"My positive attitude is my greatest strength. I can manage difficult situations in a positive manner and never let the situation take control of me instead. There was this time in my school, when two of my classmates were arguing over a simple matter. I handled the situation very carefully and established peace between them. I am really sure that I can become a great call centre executive with my positive attitude."*

### For Change of Job

*"To talk about my biggest strength, it is the willingness to take on challenges. I am looking to change my job because I have gained all the professional experience that I could gain from my current job. Moreover, there is no scope*

*of promotion left. Therefore, in order to grow even higher in my career I am looking for a new job where there are more responsibilities and scope of improvement."*

### For a Senior Level Position

*"I think that problem solving is one of my greatest strength. I analyze the situation from all angles and arrive at the best possible solution. I can get the work done in a very quick turnaround even if there are any kinds of obstacles in my way. Adding to the list, my communication skills are also top notch and often, I have received compliments from the employers working under me about my excellent communication skills that leave them with no doubt in explanation. For example, I was given a product to describe and write a report on. I analyzed the product well and used it practically to understand it better. When the final report was prepared, my boss was extremely pleased with the work I had done. I have a lot of experience as a programmer in my career, due to which I have an instinct of a developer, which I am majorly respected upon."*

*"One of my biggest strength has to be my strong work ethic. Often I have seen myself working day and night to complete the work on a given deadline. Also, I do not compromise with the quality and the final results are always in their best form. For example, there was a situation last month, where a few numbers got late from our team in Hong-Kong. I spent my weekend working on the spreadsheet because I knew that the client was expecting the spreadsheet by Monday."*

*"My writing skills are my biggest strength and I am sure that I will become a good analyst. I have the ability to communicate cumbersome niches to many different audiences. I also have the ability to process a large amount of data and that too in a very short time."*

## Make a List of Improvements and Solutions

This was all about your strengths, but there are many interviews where instead of just strengths, they ask about your weaknesses too.

Managing your strengths is still into the limit, but major cases in history tell us that candidates make biggest interview blunders while answering about their weaknesses. They absolutely have not put any effort into this and have no clue as to what to say when they are questioned about their weaknesses.

"According to Melissa Llarena, a career coach, around 90% of the candidates, even the most prepared ones, fall down to their knees when they are asked about their weaknesses." In an interview the question can be thrown at you in any package, for example, "What would your current employer have to say about your areas of improvements?" Or "Is there anything that you need to learn about this job?"

Some encourage you to go confidently and reply by saying that you are perfect and you have no weakness at all, while some suggest that not replying or saying don't know can also get you out of the situation. Anything you will say will get you out of the situation, but after getting out of that situation, are you still on the positive or negative side of the interviewer's mind?

> *"According to Melissa Llarena, a career coach, around 90% of the candidates, even the most prepared ones, fall down to their knees when they are asked about their weaknesses."*

In order to answer these questions best, talk about something that is obvious and is clearly visible in your resume, like a certificate or a certain qualification. If you have nothing as such, then talk about something that you have previously experienced and you know the way out of it. The hiring manager here is basically trying to figure out if there is a quality in you that might be critically against the job or the company. Also, this could be a question to filter the pool and only leave the golden fishes in.

It is observed that the reason for the candidates to fail in answering the weakness question is because of the following reasons

- Trying too much to convince that your weaknesses does not matter
- Refusing to answer the question
- Talking about the weakness that should not be revealed

Few examples of the answers that are relevant to the question are mentioned below:

*"Sometimes, there may be a situation where I become very impatient. This only triggers when my teammates or colleagues do not submit the work on time, which might be very critical for the on-going project. For example, I would like to mention the time when I strictly lectured one of my teammates because he didn't complete the work in time and due to him the whole project was on hold."*

*"I might be a bit confused in the situations which are just too complicated for me to handle and I might need some assistance then. Since I am a recent graduate, I still have lot to progress and learn in this field and any type of feedback and advice is taken in a very positive manner. For example, there was a situation during my internship when I didn't know how to follow Accrual Basis accounting method. I was very confused and eventually had to ask help from the seniors."*

## Study the Company

You have to research and know as much as possible about the faculty that wants to hire you. Find each and every record you can and connect the dots. Make sure the company is legitimate and has no dark history behind. If possible try contacting one of the employees working there and ask for some inside information. "Most of the candidates do not think too deep and are just happy about the opportunity. Those candidates are the ones that are unable to answer, when the questions about the organization like "What do you think about our organization?" or "Why should you be a part of this organization?" or "Tell us something about this organization", are asked. Be responsible and do your homework."

> **"Most of the candidates do not think too deep and are just happy about the opportunity. Those candidates are the ones that are unable to answer, when the questions about the organization like "What do you think about our organization?" or "Why should you be a part of this organization?" or "Tell us something about this organization", are asked."**

Rajat Sharma, son of a teacher in my organization was attending an interview few months ago. He was a recent graduate and the hiring firm was a reputed one and was only looking to hire the best candidates. Just like the other candidates, Rajat was also asked to share whatever he knew about the firm. He was prepared for this question and with his research he was able to give a somewhat different answer than what the other candidates had given already. The hiring managers were impressed with his extra knowledge that was different from the "about us" section on the website, which was the answer told by many candidates and was selected for the job.

An example of the answer is given below.

*"Since its inception, your company has maintained its reputation. It has an excellent work culture and a strong history to support the core. I am surprised by the fast growth of your company from a small number of employees to an international reach. It provides a platform for everyone to grow and I would like to be a part of it so that I can learn and gain as much*

*professional experience as possible."*

Just like Rajat, you have to research a bit more than what is available on the company's website to stand out in the eyes of the employers.

> ***"Employers are always looking for something new and different that could make a difference in their company. Just a little bit more effort can make you become that difference in any company that you are applying for."***

## Make a List of Expected Questions and Possible Answers

Every candidate has to make a list of the possible questions that could be asked in the interview. List as many questions as possible and write their answers along with them. Refine those answers as many times as possible until and unless they are in the best possible form.

This is a simple step and makes a huge difference during an interview. Imagine a situation where you are attending an exam. Few days before the exam, you receive all the questions that are appearing in the paper. Obviously, just like any other person, you will practice only those questions that are appearing in the exam and leave the rest of the syllabus. And when the exam commences, you will nail the exam very easily.

Similar to the situation above, making a list of possible answers gives you the power and confidence to nail the question when asked in an interview. The more you practice, the better answer you will be able to give and the better influence it will have on the interviewer. There are many possible questions that can be asked in an interview, a few examples are given below

- Tell me something about yourself?

- Why do you think you are a fit for this job?
- What are your biggest weaknesses?
- What do you know about this organization?
- Do you have any experience in this role?
- Why are you seeking for a new job?
- Why are you better than the candidates waiting outside?
- Do you have any questions regarding the job?
- What are your salary expectations?

These are a few questions which are very commonly asked in a job interview. Further details about the common questions asked in an interview are given later in this book.

When it comes to answers, a few possible answers to the questions above can be written as follows. The answer may differ depending upon the job you are applying for, but the basic concept of highlighting your positive points should be the main focus in every answer.

### *"Why do you think you are fit for this job?*
*I have applied for the position of a Team Leader. After working as a Call Centre Executive for five years, I have learnt how each member of a team can contribute to the overall goals of the company and have also trained and developed several team members for which my efforts were appreciated a lot.*

### *"What are your salary expectations?*
*I expect a standard salary that is given to a fresher candidate in this position. I do not have any fancy expectations as of now, because learning and growing is my main task in hand."*

### *"Do you have any questions regarding this job?*
*I would like to know, if appointed for this job, whom will I be reporting to and what will be my key performance indicators.*

## Make a List of Questions You Plan to Ask

After all the questions that the interviewer wants to ask, it will be your turn to ask them questions. This is your chance to shine and you have to ask only the relevant questions to the hiring manager. If you ask anything that is already given on the company's website, you are losing marks. Asking relevant questions can also give you an upper hand in getting the job.

> *One can come up with his or her own set of questions, provided that the questions are completely relevant and do not waste the time of the hiring managers.*

Asking the questions to the interviewer in an interview is a very important part of the interview. It is unprofessional that many do not even know about it. One should always have a list of questions that he or she can ask during an interview. As a matter of fact, the hiring managers prefer candidates who ask them questions because it gives an idea of the candidate being determined and is really passionate about the job. How hard could it be to ask "May I clear a few doubts about the post I am applying for?"

One can come up with his or her own set of questions, provided that the questions are completely relevant and do not waste the time of the hiring managers.

It is important not to forget that an interview is a two way process and asking questions in an interview, does make a difference. After all the questions are asked to you, go ahead and clear the doubts that grow at the back of your head about the job. Anything you are uncertain of, just ask it. You need to be absolutely sure about the role you are going to play for the company.

If you do not ask the right questions at the right time, you may find yourself on an uncomfortable seat spending most of your time digging through the paperwork and cursing the company and the boss. Do not forget, this situation was brought upon you by you and there is nothing you can do to undo it except finding a new job. Instead of realizing the damage in the end, ask the questions that itch you and you might be safe from a situation that is not meant for you.

Asking the right questions will not only get your doubts about the job clear, but will also leave a positive image in the eyes of the hiring managers as someone who is truly professional. What you actually need to do is to first prioritize your questions based on the interview situation, whether it is the first interview you are attending or the second one. Always try to ask open ended questions, which are the best questions you can ask an interviewer.

Make sure to have a list of questions that you want to ask at the end of the interview, the more the better. Also, ask only the questions which are relevant and only the ones you want the answer for.

So, now you know that asking questions to the interviewer is important, but what should be asked? I have compiled a few set of questions that can be asked to the hiring manager.

- What is the possible joining date, if I get selected?
- When will I get the joining letter?
- Are there any final requirements that I need to complete?
- Will I be going through any training if I get selected?
- What are the performance expectations for this job and will it change in the future?
- Can you explain me a bit about the working atmosphere here?
- How will you measure my leadership responsibilities and performance?
- Was this position recently introduced? If no, how long it has been since this position existed?
- Can you give me a brief explanation of your organization structure?

- What is the total strength of this company?
- Do I have to travel a lot?
- Who will be my working partner?
- Can you help me understand the company's management style?

*Types of questions to strictly avoid*

1. Asking about salary and benefits related to the job.
2. Questions about the company, whose information is already available on the website.
3. Avoid obvious questions like, *"When was the company founded? Or who was the founder of the company?* You can find these details very easily with some research.
4. Avoid asking questions that cannot be answered by the interviewer. *"Can you tell me if there was any case related to corruption in this company? Was there any employee who betrayed the organization?* These are very sensitive subjects and indicate the dark parts of the company. Hiring managers are proud about their company and do not like to talk about the downfalls.
5. Irrelevant questions that have no relation to the job or organization. *"Are any of your relatives also working in the company? Is there any other parking place that belongs to the company's office?"*

## Mirror Practice and Mock Practice

Practice makes a man perfect! You must have heard this term often in your life, this is true. You need practice and only practice can give you the edge you need to nail the interview. After listing all the possible question and answers that you will be asked by the interviewer and all the questions that you are going to ask the hiring manager, do a lot of practice.

You can divide the practice sessions in two categories.

- Mirror practice

- Mock practice

Mirror practice is nothing but a form of self practice. All you need to do is to sit or stand in front of the mirror and repeat the questions and answers that you have prepared loud and clear. You can try different tones and expression, which you think might be the best in that situation. The key to mirror practice is to do it genuinely. This boosts your confidence and helps effective communication.

Similarly, mock practice is also a type of practice, but here you ask someone you know to act like a hiring manager and ask you questions, which you will reply with the answers you have prepared. Just ask any of your friends or family members to assume the position of the hiring manager and ask him/her to ask the list of questions you have prepared. Basically you are creating a scenario of the interview to see how you will react in each situation. The better you do at mock practices, the better you will be able to do at the real interview. You can also try different tones and expressions you have been trying individually and see if it fits the situation.

Do not take the practice sessions lightly and commit the simple blunders that are not supposed to be done. I repeat once again, *"Practice makes a man perfect"*.

## Sufficient Number of Copies of Resume and Logistics

Never forget to carry copies of resume. You never know when you need one, just in case. Always carry a notepad and a pen along with you. Keep the sufficient number of copies of resume with you. Make sure they are printed on a good quality paper and there are no mistakes.

One should know that unprofessional resumes or paperwork is the base reason for 76% of the candidates getting rejected. Paperwork is very important. Everything you are can be determined by the relevant paper. Collect all you need beforehand, do not waste time and hurry in the end. There are many cases, where the candidates are rejected because they forget a relevant document. Interviewers have a very keen eye and like an eagle, they see it all. They know exactly where you are wrong and what your weaknesses are.

In a professional file, place extra copies of your resume, your notes for reference, your profile information, your relevant documents and also a portfolio with samples that are acceptable. Do not forget to bag in a notepad and a pen to note down any relevant information that might be useful in the future.

When it comes to logistics, be absolutely sure about the time and venue of the interview. In fact, go and visit the venue a few days prior to the interview to make sure you know where it is. Confirm the time and date and reach the venue 15 minutes before the interview to make the best impression.

Your entire interview can be easily covered in these categories, if there is enough effort put.

# CHAPTER 3

# Dressing for Success

Wherever you go, your dressing and grooming sense creates your first impression. You'll have to look professional no matter what. It is extremely important to dress in a pleasing manner. The first impression you will make on the interviewer after entering the room will be through your dressing and grooming. It is said that even though the interview duration is 10-40 minutes, the employer figures out if the candidate will be hired or not in the first 90 seconds. Therefore, creating a good first impression is of utmost importance. Every interview has its own dress code, but few general guidelines are extremely important to follow while getting dressed up for an interview. Different things are desired from men and women; hence the guidelines are different too.

Let's say for men, wearing a dark colored suit with matching trousers and light colored dressed shirt and dressed shoes with matching socks is the best option. Make sure that you are comfortable in the suit. The more comfortable you are the more confident you will be and the better you can act. Clothes should obviously be wrinkle free and neatly ironed. If you don't have an iron, borrow it or get your dress pressed one night before and hang it safely. Brush your teeth and have a proper bath. Apply deodorant to smell nice, but try avoiding cologne or aftershave, which smells too strongly. Avoid loud and hard colors for a tie and whatever color you choose, it should not be too flashy. Do your hair properly and keep it neat, clean and conservative. Shave on the morning of the interview and if you maintain a proper full beard then make sure you trim it properly so it looks clean. Your shoes should be shining and should match with your belt. These sure sound too much, but these are very small things that add up to big bonus.

Once, a student from my society applied for an interview. He was a very bright student with good academic grades. He was good behaviour wise too and always spoke very politely. The next time I met him in the park and was keen to know the results. I was expecting a very bright answer; however, he looked down and told me that he was rejected. When I pressed him to share the reason, he bluntly answered that his shirt was not pressed and had wrinkles on it. You must be thinking that it was a very simple reason to lose a talented candidate. True indeed, however, today's organizations want nothing less than perfection. There is no second chance and no excuse for failure.

Men have to have a gentleman look for an interview, however when it comes to women the idea shifts to a different level. It is better for female candidates to plan their dressing a week before the interview. There are so many things that are needed to be taken care of and anything small like wearing a funky hairclip or smelling hair oil can risk the entire interview.

Generally it is advised for a girl to wear a suit with matching pants or skirt. The suit should be comfortable and should not cause any kind of trouble during the interview. Dark colors are recommended and wearing anything too flashy and bright may seem too casual for an interview. There are many occasions when the interviewers complained about the length of the skirt, being too short or too long which may be inappropriate. Knee lengths are the best choice. Pick something conservative for blouse and avoid anything bright, animal printed, lacy, low cut and sheer. Also, keep the makeup and nail polish simple and understated, shades which are neutral to the skin are preferred. Even the jewellery and hair accessories should be less and anything funky or flashy should be absolutely avoided. Do not put on any unnecessary rings and wear only the ones which you feel are really important.

When it comes to shoes, avoid wearing anything with an open toe or back. It is probably best not to consider the shoes or sandals that you wear for the clubs and parties. Pumps are considered best to impress the interviewers, which may cost you first but is only a one time investment. You have to keep in mind that you need to dress appropriately according to the position you are applying.

The rest of the guidelines are similar to that of men's, which include keeping the outfit neat, clean and pressed. Take a shower on the morning of the interview; avoid taking head bath as you don't want your hair to be wet or sticky before an interview. Smell good with a deodorant and avoid anything that is too powerful to the nose like perfume. Keep your mouth fresh and avoid eating anything smelly during breakfast. Keep your hair clean, dry and tie it up appropriately.

The idea is to look polished and professional, not to advertise what a creative genius your hairdresser is. Focus on dressing for the job you want to have. Whatever you wear for the interview makes a lot of difference and the way you dress for an interview always matters. Always dress for success, do not let your dressing habit ruin a golden opportunity of having a good job. You need to remember that the first thing the interviewer sees, when you first enter the room, is your dress. Your many years of experience into the role and many skills you possess will always be judged after you are judged on the clothes you are wearing.



Getting the job depends on many factors which are beyond your control and you never know what the interviewer actually wants and his sense of judgment. You cannot control the employer's thoughts, perceptions, preferences or the number of competitors that are there to get the job. However, you are completely responsible for how you dress and how you maintain your image in front of them. Dressing properly can send a very powerful message to the hiring managers and can also indicate them if you are a potential candidate for the job or not.

I repeat; it is extremely important to dress according to the role you are applying for. If you are applying to wait tables in a coffee shop and if you are applying for a law firm, the dressing manner in both the cases will be completely different. The best way to find out a proper dress is to ask an employer working there or just wait for sometime outside the organization and you will at least get a brief idea how to dress for the interview.

Just as I mentioned before, everything you are wearing matters, even the color of the tie you are wearing matters. According to research, the color you wear for an interview actually matters. Different colors are known to evoke different emotions and it is extremely important to evoke the right emotions from the hiring managers. Do not take the colors lightly, choose your colors carefully. The significance of colors is given below to give you a brief understanding of their emotional effects.

**Blue:** Blue is the color of the sky and ocean. It is commonly associated with trust, wisdom, peace, and loyalty. If you are wearing blue, may be a very important gesture could be made in an interview. Portraying all the qualities that are needed to be displayed in an interview, blue is the choice made by many interviewees to impress the hiring managers. If you are wearing blue, indicates that you are honest and loyal towards the work. Also, studies have proved that wearing blue to an interview increases your chance of getting hired.

**Red:** Red is known for its fiery and emotional effects. Red color brings out the fiery emotions which can work against you in an interview. Being a very strong and extreme color, it is recommended by many not to wear red to an interview. Unlike the color blue, which is known for its calming effects, red can prove to be a very intimidating color for an interview.

**Orange:** I would recommend that you avoid wearing orange to an interview. The reason is, just like the color red; orange is also known for its effects on stirring emotion and can be too intimidating. Although, orange is still calmer than the color red, it still can evoke very powerful feelings and emotions.

**Grey:** Grey is considered as the second most favorite color to wear in an interview. With its qualities of bringing out the professional and confident you, grey can be a very effective colour without being intimidating on the interviewer. Grey gives you the sophisticated and authoritative look, which might give you a plus point during an interview.

**Black:** Wearing black to an interview is the most preferred option. However, most of the candidates ignore the fact that black is a very powerful color and wearing entirely black outfit can be considered as arrogant. Black is also combined with negative emotions like sin, fear and death. Therefore, have a good combination to wear with black so that the effect is balanced.

# CHAPTER 4

# Two Secrets That Determine 93% of Interview Success

Since my childhood, I was able to understand what the person's mood is by looking at his facial expression and behaviour. I understood when someone was lying and hiding the truth. Later on, this ability gave me an upper hand in many interviews, where I was in charge. Many candidates give themselves away with their body language; they speak different words than what can be read in their eyes.

It is extremely important to understand the environment. As soon as you enter the room the interviewer may signal you to sit down using his or her hand and you may fail to notice. This may be very simple to you, but then the interviewer has to say things out loud and no interviewer likes to repeat things, which is a fact. You have to be a good observer.

*"The first thing after entering the room should be to*

My friend's son was attending an interview recently. He had just finished his degree and was applying for a job in some private firm. He narrated his experience at the interview at a social gathering. He told me that just like most of the interviews, there were only three positions and twenty candidates competing for them. One thing that was extremely surprising was that all the 20 candidates were assessed in just two hours of time. I couldn't stop my curiosity and asked him what happened when he entered the room.

He replied that as he entered the room there was three middle-aged men seated around a large table. The table was large so a handshake was not possible. They gestured him to sit and asked general questions about his life, like where was the graduation done and a little bit about his family. There was not a single question related to the firm or the job. He was done in just five minutes and asked to wait till the results were announced. After waiting for another hour, results were announced and his name was included. He was very happy with the fact that he got the job and that too without putting much effort.

I was not at all satisfied and wanted to figure out the reason behind this mysterious interview. Luckily I knew one of the three interviewers from a new year's party three years ago. I somehow connected the dots finally leading to him and enquired about this brainstorming reality. He took a pause for a second and revealed that he and his partners were just deciding whom to hire by observing the candidate's body language. The candidates that did not make eye contact were rejected instantly, while a few more were rejected because they couldn't hide their stress and anxiousness, which are two main signs of weaknesses. He also explained that the candidates who were selected were very confident and maintained eye contact while speaking as well as while listening. Their hands were very professional and the body posture was properly maintained. The main aim of the firm was to hire employees, who were confident and hid their weaknesses effectively. The rest of the details are already present in the resume and training was obvious upon hiring, so, they did not care about anything else other than the person's personality, which they judged on the basis of the body language.

> *"The candidates that did not make eye contact were rejected instantly, while a few more were rejected because they couldn't hide their stress and anxiousness, which are two main signs of weaknesses."*

This incident always rang a bell inside my head and I never miss an opportunity to explain the new trainees to observe and understand the important signs and gestures needed for an interview. It is not hard to figure out someone's body language, all you need is the knowledge and some application. I am sure that you can easily figure out your dad's and mom's mood when you have done something wrong and you didn't tell them yet or you went somewhere and you did not come back. Those times are tough and you already know what the results are.

Similarly, if you figure out the mood of the interviewers, there is a high possibility that you can figure out the twists and turns during an interview. You can figure out your parent's mood easily because you know them well and you understand their expressions. However, in this case you need to apply logic. There are some basic steps that you can follow to get a better understanding of the interviewer's mood.

- Look at the expression of the interviewer as soon as you enter the room. Most of the interviewers are experienced and show no signs of emotion, but sometimes if you are lucky you might understand the mood just with the facial expression.
- Let the interviewer speak first. Do not speak until asked. Generally, the first question sets the complete atmosphere for the rest of the interview. If the first question asked to you is direct and on the topic like, "why do you think you are fit for this job?" or "Tell us why you are a good candidate for this job", then the mood is serious and the interviewer is expecting you to react quick and give quick answers.
- If the first question is casual like, "How are you?" or "We are pleased to see you, tell us something about yourself", then you can expect a casual interview. However, a casual interview is considered much more challenging than a straight forwarded one as a casual interview generally involves a lot of tricky questions, which require the candidates to put in a lot of logic.

- Observe the tone of the interviewer and try to figure out his or her emotions through that. If the interviewer's voice is loud and pressing, then you are in for a rough time. But, most of the interviewers try to put you at ease first and then suddenly put you in a difficult situation to see your potential.

*"Keeping eye contact while speaking signifies that you are confident and saying the truth. Moreover, keeping eye contact while listening makes you a good listener, who is concentrated and focused."*

Always remember to make eye contact while speaking and also do not break eye contact while listening. Looking at the walls or out of the window while speaking or listening can land you up in either of the places. Also, keep your back straight and sit formally. Many individuals are confused about where to keep their hands during an interview. It is considered best to keep them in your lap and formally lock them with each other. While you are speaking, move your hands along with the dialogues. Place your hands still while not speaking and do not touch your nose, mouth, ear or any other parts of the body too much. Maintain the decorum inside the interview room.

According to a research the second most important factor that leads to failure in interviews is lack of enthusiasm and confidence that the candidate shows in the interview. The primary reason for that is very low level of voice and lack of voice modulation. Now you may want to know what Voice Modulation is. How does it impact an interview?

Let me share with you some very important information about Voice Modulation that I have been sharing in my Voice Modulation Workshops in Mumbai. Well, voice communicates a lot about our current state of excitement and confidence. Since I have trained over 250,000 professionals, I have observed that 98% of students and working professionals do not modulate their voice. And because of this reason, they are perceived as people who lack confidence.

Now in an interview, your hiring manager is continuously judging your personality and if your voice does not show confidence, the interviewer will be unsure of hiring you. In order to develop a high quality voice, one must follow the following tips:

- Do loud reading practise for 30 minutes daily – this will help you open up your voice.
- In case people around you complain that you speak very fast, you need to accept that you are speaking more than 150 words per minute. Generally when you speak 100 words per minute, it is very easy to understand what you are saying. In order to speak at a rate that the interviewer can easily understand what you are saying, practise extremely slow reading. Read text with a five second gap between two words. You need to do this for 30 minutes daily. Thousands of professionals have used this technique to drastically reduce their rate of speech.
- Learn to correctly modulate your voice. When you modulate your voice, it makes your speech interesting; it helps you express your emotions and also creates an impression that you are confident. In order to develop modulation in your voice, underline two three words in each sentence. Now read the text loudly and stress on the underlined words. Do this for 30 minutes daily. This will help you develop voice modulation.
- Record your speech on voice recorder on your mobile phone. Then listen to it. Don't be surprised if you are not very comfortable with your voice. This happens with a lot of people. Now follow the above tips and then record your voice again and listen. Do this till you are satisfied with the quality of your voice.
- Give your voice some rest before interview. This will help you to speak with energy in the interview.
- Gargle with warm water and salt daily. This will clear your

throat.

# CHAPTER 5

# Behavioural and Situational Interview



I t is said that past behaviour is a better predictor of future behaviour. The fact that actually amazes everyone and also puts a huge weight on this topic is that 80% of the interview is made up of behavioural questions. It is important to understand what behavioural questions are before we move on to know how to answer them. The behavioural questions are included in your interview in order to get a preview of your future actions using the examples from your past. Therefore, your behaviour in certain situations in previous job can be a reliable indicator of what your actions will be in the future.

*"80% of the interview is made up of behavioural*

If set out to find the types of behavioural questions, you can literally count to thousands and more. In this case, the best way to prepare for the behavioural question is to research the organization and list out the behavioural traits that are essential to working in that particular organization. There is quite a bit of difference between the behaviour type questions and the standard interview questions, as the former focuses majorly on your experiences, skills, abilities, knowledge and behaviours. Therefore, instead of a standard interview question, which is "Do you have leadership skills?" a behavioural question will be more like "Share an experience which illustrates your leadership qualities."

The skills necessary for the job are already given by the interviewer, so it is extremely important that you come prepared to answer these questions in the best way possible. I suggest that to begin with, go through the job description and list out the skills that are required for the job. It is more likely that the interviewer will focus on the skills mentioned in the job description than the skills which are not. For example, if the job description has mentioned "good teamwork skills" and "advertising skills", then you can expect behavioural questions depending on these skills to analyze if you really possess them or not. According to me, these questions are the most scoring ones in an interview and if prepared properly, you could easily impress the hiring managers.

During the interview, you are asked, "Provide any instance where you set a milestone and successfully achieved it." Obviously, here you have to provide any live instance where you actually achieved a milestone. Present a story and convince the hiring managers that it is true. Sounds simple, doesn't it? However, situational or behavioural questions are quite tricky to answer. You'll never know where you made a mistake and if the hiring managers noticed it. Since, it is a story, you could make any simple mistake and the HR managers could easily notice it.

## STAR format

To answer the behavioural questions, it is recommended that you use the STAR format.

**S- Situation-** The interviewer expects to hear about a challenge or a situation that you faced recently.

**T- Task-** The interviewer would like to understand what was your main objective in that situation.

**A- Action-** You will have to tell the hiring managers, the steps you took to achieve that objective and the reason behind your actions.

**R- Result-** Then you have to share the final results of your actions and did you achieve your objective and if yes, then how your actions helped in achieving the objective. What did you learn from that situation and did you apply the learning anywhere else?

This formula is hugely recommended by professional interviewers and hiring managers to get a straight detailed answer instead of any cooked story. So if you were asked the above question, you can answer in the following manner.

**Situation-** Since I was a project manager, my role in the company was to make sure that the projects are completed on time and within the given budget.

**Task-** There was a time recently when my hands were full as I had a job of combining three office spaces in one. I had the deadline of 90 days and I was sure that with many other contracts in process, it would be a hard struggle to finish the job in time. However, I set the deadline of 80 days, so that the last 10 could be left for revisions and corrections in the end.

**Action-** I applied the logic of classification and divided the contractors into three main teams. Then I assigned three project managers to control these three teams. This allowed me to create an effective work timetable and ensure that the workload was kept to a minimum.

**Result-** The implemented idea worked excellently and we were finally able to finish the job within deadline and also reduced costs by 15%. The simple idea of dividing the contractors into smaller teams was widely appreciated and is now being implemented into standard work procedure, which has proven to be very effective and overall cost reducing.

Let us take another example in a similar way and apply the STAR formula to understand it better. Suppose the interviewer is a student or graduate and the question asked is "Share an incident in your school, when you were praised for your leadership qualities." The answer could be in the following manner.

**(Situation)** *"I was the House Captain of my House in school.* **(Task)** *There was a tension built up in the house due to some misunderstanding between our own two mates. The House was not able to focus in the House Competitions due to this fight.* **(Action)** *I figured that talking to each of them individually will help me find out the solution to the situation.* **(Result)** *After speaking to both of them, I was able to sort out the misunderstanding between them with me acting as a mediator. I did not let the tension grow further and no teachers were involved. The dispute between the two mates came to an end and the House started focusing on the right track again."*

*One can easily understand from the above two examples that it is best to* prepare a mental outline, while answering any behavioural question. Preparing genuine stories and examples that prove your skills and abilities put to use will help you answer and behavioural question with ease. Also, the authenticity of the answer depends on your confidence while answering any behavioural question.

## Six Most Common behavioural questions that you absolutely have to prepare

As you all know by now that behavioural questions are very common and important part of any interview. You have to prepare these questions with extreme caution to not miss any detail. There are hundreds of behavioural questions and it is impossible to prepare each and every one of them. Therefore, I have categorized the six most commonly asked of behavioural questions that you absolutely should prepare before going to any interview.

*Type 1: When you found a solution to a problem*

Problem solver is the skill that is included in almost every job description and resume. Anybody can just add that skill to their skill set and pose as a problem solver, but in an interview you actually have to prove your problem solving skills. Therefore, it is best to be ready and prepare a few instances where you have exercised these skills live.

You can include any situation where your involvement has resulted in solving the problem. It can be about the time when you helped two friends solve a misunderstanding between them or about the time when you had to come up with a last second decision to save the project and finish it within the set deadline.

Think deeply if you have any actual memories in the back of your mind that displays your problem solving personality that is always inside you. Also, do not talk about any simple problem you fixed, like you started keeping reserve petrol in the back of your car for emergency cases. Do a favor to yourself and keep these tidbits to yourself.

*Type 2: When you successfully completed a challenge*

Your work environment can be full of thrills. You may be having a hard time managing your relation with the boss or you may be stuck with a very tough task to complete the project, it is still very important to face a challenge when thrown at you.

If you dig back into your past, you can find so many instances where you have successfully won a challenge fair and square, but, do not lie about climbing Mount Everest or living in a jungle for a week just to taste the wildlife, be simple and do not create a movie plot in an interview.

Instead, try narrating a real life instance from your life when you faced a challenge and you did everything in your power to overcome that challenge. You can talk about how you worked at a very less paying part-time job to pay your college fees or maybe about the time where you met the work deadline when it was impossible to do so. These simple stories are enough to get you around the behavioural corner and continue the interview smoothly.

*Type 3: When you commit a mistake*

It is obvious that no one is perfect and your interviewers are well aware of the fact that you are not perfect either. But the important part here is that the interviewers wants to know if you actually learn something out of the mistake or just let it pass.

There could be many instances of you making mistakes in your life, it won't be hard to prepare a dropdown of them, and however, you have to be very selective about which one to share with the hiring managers. Do not talk about a mistake that is extremely stupid and was a total waste of time.

Instead, talk about something genuine, but small and briefly explain what were the steps taken by you to solve the issue. It is very important to understand that the mistake is not the centre of attention here, but the steps that you took immediately after to solve the problem and what did you learn from it.

### Type 4: When you were the leader

Any job interview will have questions related to your leadership skills. Moreover, if the post you are applying for is a managerial position, you will have to ensure beforehand to have a few examples of your leadership skills in your bag.

Talk about how your leadership skills lead the whole team to be the best in the company or about the time when you have to solve a fight between two teammates, or talking about how you motivate your entire sports team. Just let the interviewers know that you have the experience of being a leader and you can manage the job.

The best way to answer these questions is to briefly explain the situation and tell them how your decisions affected the results in a positive manner. Always have a few examples ready, when it comes to leadership qualities.

### Type 5: When you had a team to work with

It is obviously inevitable that you have to share working time with others. Therefore, you definitely have to focus on teamwork qualities. Your interviewers would like to understand if you would be able to work with a team and also do not disrupt the working environment.

You can come up with so many examples, when it comes to the talk about teamwork. You may have all the memories when you teamed up with your friends or family members to achieve an objective. Similarly, talk about the situations where you teamed up with your classmates or colleagues to finish a very difficult project which had a short deadline. It is extremely important to make the interviewer understand that you know how to socialize and work with a team, also make sure that you make them understand that you know the true value of teamwork.

So, the next time you attend an interview, pick something up from your memory reel in which you teamed up with others and performed well.

*Type 6: When you did something interesting and different*

Obviously, interview is mostly about finding out if you are fit for the job and if you are qualified to work effectively. But, if you impress your interviewer brilliantly, you can expect the questions which are personal too as the hiring manager would like to know you more. If they think you are a very potential fit then they will go the extra mile to know more about you.

It won't be too good if you just stare the interviewer blankly when he or she wants to conclude the interview with the words, "Tell me about what you like to do after the office hours."

So when, the question is asked, you should be prepared to let out the answer in the most confident way. Even if you are attending cooking classes these days or learning how to drive, you should be able to impress the hiring manager with a good answer for this question. Not only the answer will boost your impression, but also will leave the hiring manager to associate something with your name.

Behavioural questions in an interview can be a bit tricky and can go either ways, but they are also a perfect opportunity to let the hiring managers know what you are actually capable of and that you are truly determined to get the job.

## Extensive list of behavioural questions in an interview:

- Tell us about the time when you had work overload and how did you overcome the situation.
- Share with us a difficult decision that you had to make last year.
- Give me an example of the situation where you had failed to complete the work in time.
- Give me an example of the situation, where you volunteered to lead the project.
- Share with us an incident from your life, where you had to

manage an unhappy customer.

- Give me an instance where you motivated your teammates, which helped the outcome of the project.
- Share an example of a situation where you set a goal and what actions you took to achieve the goal.
- Talk to us about an unsupported decision you made and how you handled it.
- Tell us about the time when you used your negotiation skills to change a customer's opinion.
- Describe a situation when you had very less time and had to make a quick decision.
- Have you ever come across a situation where you knew that your boss was wrong? How did you handle it?
- Describe the situation where you used your insightful judgment in solving problems.
- Explain us about a major change in your job and what were your reactions to the change?
- Talk to us about the time when you were forced to make changes and adjust accordingly. What were the steps taken by you to handle the change?
- Describe a situation in your career when you were successfully able to point out an error to your supervisor.
- Did you have any experience of facing a conflict at your place? If yes, then how did you handle the situation?
- Tell us about the most difficult decision you had to make in the last six years and what made the decision so difficult?
- Provide an example of your actions where in order to get the work done you had to go beyond your normal duties.
- Provide an example of the situation where you put your teammate's needs in front of your own needs while completing a task.
- Describe a situation where your knowledge and skills enhanced the outcome significantly.
- Tell us about the situation, where you encountered problems with

your co-workers or boss and what did you do to resolve the issue.

- Tell us about a stressful situation you faced recently and what was your reaction to the pressure?
- Tell us about the situation where you were able to motivate a teammate or a co-worker.
- Tell us about the time when you were able to have a positive influence on your workmates.
- Tell us a situation where you had very little guidance and yet you finished the work successfully.
- Describe a situation when you were able to achieve a goal with your team.
- Tell us about the time when you had to adapt to a different work environment.
- Have you ever gone out of your way to help someone feel comfortable in the work environment?
- Talk to us about the most effective decision you made as a part of a special team or task group.
- Tell us about the team experience that was rewarding.
- Describe a team experience where you were disappointed with the results.
- Have you faced any stressful situation? What did you do to deal with it?
- Have you ever faced difficulties in your work environment to get others accept your ideas? How did you deal with it?
- Tell us if you have ever worked with conflicting deadlines and how you did decide which task to be completed first.
- Tell us about a very complex problem you faced recently.
- Do you have any past work experience where you have made reliable contribution to the team environment?
- Did you have any annoying or un-popular co-worker to deal with? If yes, how did you deal with that person?
- Describe a situation where you went overtime on your deadline.
- Describe a situation when you understood the situation wrong and made a wrong decision. What did you do to fix it?

- Describe a situation where you had to delegate a task.
- Have you ever had a situation where you were unsure how to proceed, but were too afraid to ask for help.
- Give us an example of how you had to use different management skills for different people in your work environment.
- Give an example where you were able to promote morale in your work environment.
- What has been the biggest contribution you made in your current role and why?
- What is the thing that you are most proud of in your working career?
- Did you ever face difficulty pleasing a customer? What did you do to make sure the customer is happy?
- When was the last time you had to face constructive criticism by your supervisor and what was your reaction to that?
- Tell us about a setback you have overcome in past 12 months.
- Discuss a situation where you found out that someone was dishonest to you and how was the situation sorted out.

## Situational Questions

Hiring managers never take risks while hiring someone new. Therefore, you have to sit a little longer on your desk than expected to learn the tricks behind situational questions. Now, situational questions are just a bit different then behavioural questions.

*"Behavioural questions are asked based on your past experiences and your actions that helped overcome those situations, whereas situational questions are hypothetical questions which are asked to test your analyzing skills and reaction timing."*

You are given a situation and you have to analyze it and find a most suitable solution to the situation, which would be best for the company. Just like a game where one would give you a puzzle and you have to find a solution to that puzzle, situational questions are very similar too. Just instead of one particular answer, there are many different answers depending upon how you analyze the question. You have to give the best answer because the interviewers judge your actions according to your answers if a similar situation is to arise in the company.

A few examples of situational questions are:

- How will you react if you found out that an employee is stealing from the business?
- What will you do if you are asked to do something unethical by your supervisors?
- How will you handle the situation when you have a deadline and you are running out of time?
- What measures will you take to handle an employee who is disturbing the work environment?
- Imagine you have a manager's position, how will you handle the heavy workload when you have staff shortage?
- How will you react when your supervisor makes a decision that you do not agree upon?
- What measures will you take to motivate a team member, if he is not contributing towards a project?
- What steps you will take as a manager to build team spirit?

Since, there are quite a number of ways to answer a situational question; it is hard to understand which one is the best. It is important to remember that situational questions are just hypothetical and does not necessarily involve past experiences, therefore, the best way to prepare these answers is to follow simple rules that will give you the idea to prioritize your answers.

**Rule 1:** It is important to be prepared and understand the role completely which you are applying for. By knowing what your role actually is, you can figure out most of the questions that are going to be asked by the interviewer. Take an example of managerial position, and then the question can be "What steps you will take as a manager to build team spirit?" If you understand the role you are applying for and the company offering the job, it is more likely for you to have a brief idea of the situational questions coming your way.

**Rule 2:** While preparing for your interview, make a list of the events from your past job where your actions and decisions lead to a positive outcome. Supposedly, if you are a fresh graduate then gather your personal experiences like volunteering work or any other club memberships you have.

**Rule 3:** Create genuinely convincing stories of your actions that were appreciated and how those actions helped solve the problem in hand. It is very important that your actions have clear understanding of how it leads to resolve the issues.

You need to understand these simple rules and apply them in the situations given by the hiring manager. Practice with sample questions or create a scenario on your own and try to find the best possible solution. The application of the rules could be understood better with a few examples.

***What will be your reaction if you found out that your team member is not contributing towards the project?***

*In a situation where one of my team members was not contributing towards the project in any manner, that was leading to a dispute within the team and the problem had to be quickly solved. I would have solved this problem with direct communication privately, where I could understand him much more easily. Most probably, these kinds of situations arise due to the team member not understanding the subject or he does not quite know what his role in the* team is. I was able to find out the reason behind the problem and later, the team members too helped us reach a solution.

## What would you do if your supervisor was taking the wrong decision?

If this situation ever arises in my presence, I would discuss my reasons openly with the senior and would provide him an alternate option to achieve his objective. It is quite unacceptable to question a senior's decision without actually providing any parameters and reasons. I would be fully prepared before I discuss my opinions with him and also, the meeting would be in private and not in front of his team members.

## How would you react if the project given to you is changed or the deadline has been suddenly shortened?

It would be my priority to first find out the reason behind the sudden changes, therefore, my first step would be to speak with the supervisor and ascertain the situation. Once, I get my facts and answers straight, I would let my team know that the changes had been made and will also announce a team meeting to discuss and develop a new strategy for the new project.

# CHAPTER 6

# Tricky Questions and their Answers

While in an interview, you are bound to come across questions, which are very tricky and can leave you speechless. The questions can be related to anything, it maybe something personal about you, it may be something about the organization; it may be a situation in which your reaction will be judged or could be something simple but practical. You have to be very quick witted in these situations and with a calm sense analyze the question from all angles. If they find any kind of weakness, there is a high risk that the rest of the interview can fall into the pit. The questions can be anything, after researching for a while I found out few questions that are very common but can leave someone in a difficult situation.

- Have you attended any interview before? If yes why didn't you get selected?
- Are you familiar with the company's history?
- Give me an example of your quick thinking?
- Have you ever handled major crisis, if yes, how?
- Would you like to have water or coffee?
- What is the company's impression on you?

- Tell us something about yourself in brief.

There are many more that can be added to the list. It is always quite difficult to answer these questions and most of the candidates cannot answer them properly, resulting in minus points. I had to brainstorm to finally write down some general tips to get these answers right. I had to come up with something called *"Five Tip Rule"* to tackle these questions, which are mentioned below.

- Tip number one, whatever your answer is, keep it positive. Everything that you say has to end in a positive tone. Most of the interviewers like the positive nature of the candidate and support them well.
- Never say a single word useless. Take your time and plan your answer. The answers always have to be short and simple. Whatever you say should cross the table and reach the listeners. Every word should be heard and understood. It is the good communication skill that matters here the most.
- The third tip is to not get emotional and fall into the trap. Professionalism is what the interviewers want. Every firm wants a candidate who is emotionally strong and can handle tough situations. If you maintain your calm senses here, it will prove to the questioners that you have the ability to handle tough situations.
- Be confident and try to provide evidence to justify it. Your story should revolve around your achievements, which you can prove that they are a reality. Everything you say has to sound real and confident. Talk loud and clear, always.
- Do not break eye contact. Always look up and into the eyes of the interviewer. Looking somewhere else may indicate lack of confidence, which can leave a negative impression. Practice the way you speak in the mirror and do not shy away while talking.

The way you speak and respond decides the major part of your interview. If your response does not have weight, it can lead to a failure. For every question, personal or related to the job, you need to answer it in a systematic manner that actually makes sense. Organize your answer in a particular order, from beginning of time to your present. For example, if the question is about your education, do not answer your qualification randomly; follow a specific date line that always take you forward. Your answer should start from your schooling and then your graduation followed by your higher qualifications if any. Include the certificate courses or your diplomas in your answer where the dates go in the same manner.

*Always look up and into the eyes of the interviewer. Looking somewhere else may indicate lack of confidence,*

The HR manager judges you in every question he asks. There are many possible ways to answer a single question and it also depends on person to person, company to company or job to job. A company with specific job openings will only recruit the person who gives the most relevant answers according to the post. Here, the candidates applying may have different qualifications, experience and background, so the answer may be different for each of them. Consider a few candidates applying for a job in a company recruiting accountants, and then the answers for each candidate will bend more towards the required field. Now consider the same candidates with the same qualification applying for a job in a different company recruiting a manager, they cannot answer the same answers here, their answers will now have to be more relevant to the manager's job instead of the accountant's.

*Let us take an example of Vishal, who applies for an accountant's post in a company. He is called for the interview and during the interview he is asked, "What are your qualities that make you suitable for the job?" Vishal answers the question very confidently, "I have a degree that is fit for this job and my academic grades are very good too. My father owns a book store and I regularly scan the numbers and find out the errors associated. This actually gave me experience and ability to manage large numbers in a quick turnaround."*

*Now, consider if Vishal wants to grow and applies for a manger's post in a well known firm. He is called for the interview and is asked the same question. Since the job he is applying for is different than what he previously applied for, he changes his answer, "I am a very patient man and have the ability to understand the worker's potential. My father owns a very reputed bookstore and I managed the shop whenever he was not around. This gave a boost to my managing abilities and I am sure that without stressing the workers, I can guide them to produce best results."*

You can observe that Vishal used his father's bookstore in both the answers, but the difference was just that he chose the role in each case differently by making the answer more relevant to the job. Similarly, same applies for every candidate applying for the interview.

This actually puts us in a difficult situation, where it is impossible to find a perfect answer for the same question asked in different interviews. However, there is a root for every question, which is same for every interview. Like in the case of Vishal, the root was his father's bookstore and he used it in both the interviews. Therefore, there are a few guidelines for every question, which provides a base for every question. Using these guidelines, one can easily create a possibly strong answer. Guidelines for most asked interview questions are given below.

## Tell me Something About Yourself

Most of the interviews begin with this question. Obviously, every candidate is prepared for this question and answers this question in the most confident manner. However, it is necessary to keep in mind here that the HR manager only wants to know the relevant details that are actually necessary, if you go on about telling your life story from the time you grew up, there is no doubt that you will soon be hunting for another job opening in some other firm.

There are many different cases observed, where the candidate talks about his or her complex past situations and how there is no peace and harmony at his or her home. There should be nothing negative in your answer as these things are not meant to be brought up in an interview voluntarily. It creates a bad image; moreover, you should only be talking about your education, qualifications and career.

There is no point speaking more than needed. Restrict your answer to only details that are relevant. Ideally one should restrict answer to this question in five sentences.

- *My name is [First Name] [Last Name]*
- *I stay in [area name]*
- *I have completed [highest qualification... instead of M. Com. Say Masters in Commerce] in [Year] from [Institute Name].*
- *Overall I have [x] years of experience and am currently working as [current designation] with [company name] since [start of the current job e.g. March 2016]*
- *My manager and colleagues have always appreciated my [top two qualities that you have and are relevant to the job you are applying for – e.g. Communication Skills, Quick Learner, Positive Approach, Attention to Detail, Teamwork, Leadership, Focus on Numbers, Accuracy, Quick Turnaround Time, Multi-task, Creativity, Dedication, Research oriented, etc]*

The interviewer will then have an opportunity to ask questions based on these points and decide the course of interview. If there is anything else that the interviewer wishes to know about you, then he or she will ask you about it. I have provided an answer to this question below, which I explained to one of my students during the "Interview Success Workshop" that I conducted in Mumbai at one of our training centers.

*A candidate once approached me and said, "Good Morning sir, as a Fresher, I am going to introducing myself in an interview. Would you help in determining if there are any errors?"*

*"Good Morning, my name is S.B. Jabeer. I am from Kadapa district which is in Andhra Pradesh. I have recently completed my Bachelor of Technology in Electronics and Communication Engineering from JNTU University. I secured 92% in my secondary education exams and 86% in matriculation. Coming to my academic projects, I have done my academic project in security camera system operating on solar energy. This system is implemented in the areas where security is significant, especially in the Banking services, vehicle parking areas and certain more areas where surveillance is essential. My*

*interpersonal skills are, I had a strong desire towards the achievement of goals and to be able to cope up with different situations and can adapt to new challenges and opportunities. My hobbies are; I would like to watch tennis and play cricket. That's all about me. Thank you very much. Have a nice day."*

I explained Jabeer that this introduction is too long and the purpose of this question is to briefly know about you. It can be answered like:

*Good Morning, My name is SB. Jabeer. I belong to Kadapa district which is in Andhra. I have completed my bachelor of technology in electronics and communication engineering from JNTU University. People who know me say that I am a determined person. That's all about me."*

## What was the reason for leaving your last job?

This is one of the trickiest questions asked in an interview. Remember; do not bad mouth your previous employer in any scenario. You have to present yourself in an utmost positive manner and there should not be any negative signs from your side. Talking bad about your old boss, company or peers is considered as extremely unprofessional and can decrease your chances of getting the job by a large margin. The best way to answer this question is to talk about career advancement and the new company which you are applying for is the right choice for you.

Answering this question can be a bit different for the ones who were fired from their previous job. If you were fired, please do not try to cover it up or lie about it in the interview. There are great chances that the company will check your background anyway, so it is better to come clean from the start. The best way to answer this question if you were fired is to keep it brief and simple. Turn your negative points into positive points by talking about how it was a learning experience for you and what did you do to make up for the mistakes then.

Talking about moving on with good confidence can give you extra points. For example, *"My skills were not too useful in my previous post. Also, my boss and I had a very different way of thinking and we decided that I should move on to a job where my skills were better used."*

## Which other companies have you applied for?

I suggest that you be relaxed when this question is asked. The main motive behind asking this question is to ensure that you are quite serious about finding a new job. If you have applied for a job in many different companies, remember not to give out the entire details, you don't want to sound too desperate and give them the idea that you will take any job available.

You need to sound professional and confident, mention one or two good companies, offering a decent salary to give them an idea that you have capabilities and you aim high. More importantly convince them that you actually are very serious in getting a new job.

## What are your strengths?

If you think of it, this question is one of the easiest questions that you might have come across. The mistake that most people make while answering this question is that, many people give very common answers. Now what does a very common answer mean? It means an answer that many or everyone usually gives- for example, "I'm pretty hardworking" or "I am very loyal to the company I work for" and so on. Your answer depends on the kind of job you're applying for. Like, if you are applying for an accountancy position, you cannot say that you are good at clerical work.

The answer that you give should ring a bell in the interviewer's mind and make him or her think that, you have something that the other applicants might not have. Use words that show that you have skills which are useful for the job that you are applying for. Avoid words and behaviour that may look or feel very generic. Let us take an example of a graphic designer answering this question:

*"As a graphic designer, my greatest strength is that I understand the need of various people and turn it into the final design work. My passion for creativity and mastery over most features of Photoshop add glitter to gold. Moreover, I can blend in with people easily and so I have great compatibility of working in a team."*

## What are your weaknesses?

Where strengths may feel like the easiest questions to answer, undoubtedly one would say that answering questions related to weaknesses is also pretty easy. No. The questions related to weaknesses are the hardest to answer.

At the same time, if you think that saying you have little to none weaknesses might give you a stand in the interview, you are extremely wrong. If you say that you have nothing that you must work on, you will come out as being very much arrogant. Speak of a weakness that will not ruin your chances of getting selected, and that can also maintain a very good impression in front of the interviewer. When they are asking your weaknesses, it is one hundred per cent work related, so do not talk of domestic weaknesses, such as helping in chores around the house and baking cakes.

These answers will sound extremely absurd and the interviewer will think that you cannot comprehend the questions and tasks given to you. If you are applying a job related to telemarketing, you can say something like you are not good at accounts or designing. Do anything but don't avoid the question. The interviewer has asked you this question, and now you will have to answer it.

The best advice would be to tell a work related weakness and then follow it up by giving examples that you can work on it. If you admit your real weakness, and convince the person in front of you that you can work on it, the interviewer can trust you more. Again, the job that you are applying for will determine the answer you give. I would like to provide an answer that I gave to one of my students Sheetal Sharma during the "Interview Success Workshop" conducted in Hyderabad a few months ago.

*She asked me "Sir, as a fresher, I have interest in Customer Service Agent for Airport. Please could you help me in tips for interview in customer service! And how shall I talk about my strength and weaknesses for this position?*

*Since I am very people friendly, I would like to work with your esteemed organization as a Customer Service Executive. I enjoy interacting with strangers and making them comfortable. This is my strength. I also enjoy any work that demands multi-tasking. Someone suggested that my English needs improvement and that is my weakness. In order to solve that, I have joined a professional English Training Course and am working on it."*

## How do you handle extremely stressful situations?

One of the most common question asked in almost all the interviews across the world is, how you deal with stress. It is obvious that you will face many stressful situations in your personal life as well as work life. The interviewer wants to know how you handle that pressure in a healthy way.

No employer would like to have an employee in his office who shouts at other employees or talks rude with the customers just because he had a rough day. Make sure you give them an idea of how positive you are and give examples of how you handled stressful situations in your real life.

You are likely to encounter many stressful situations in jobs like customer service, call centre or other jobs where you have to deal with the customers directly. Therefore, if you are applying for one of these jobs, your interviewer will most likely ask you this question in order to understand if you can cope with different kind of customers who want to enjoy all the benefits the company has to offer.

It is important to emphasize that you are a very calm and have high tolerance for stress and give relevant examples of stressful situations in which you stayed calm, managed the situation and coped up with stress in a very healthy manner.

Here are a few tips that will help you answer this question.

- Everyone has their own way of dealing with stress and often all the ways are not healthy, so mention only the positive things you do to keep your cool.
- Narrow down your answer to the stress faced at workplace and try to avoid talking about the stress you face in your personal life.
- Please do not talk about how you will stop the angry babbling customer with your own dictionary.

Example answer –

*"I usually have a very high tolerance for stressful situations and handle stress well. I try to keep my cool and understand the situation first, and then try to find a solution in a professional manner. To illustrate, once a customer was very irritated on the fact that the store's return policy was only available for 30 days and she exceeded her time limit. She was quiet loud and was also using an abusive language. However, I remained calm and carefully explained the policy and why was it placed. When I had the situation in control, I then showed her some other similar items that she could try. I believe that the only reason that the customer calmed down was because I remained calm and kept my cool."*

## Why should the company hire you for this job?

This is a very frequently asked question in most interviews. The answer is pretty simple, right? Just make the interviewer know what you already know about yourself. They should hire you because obviously you are the right one for this job! You have got to let them know about your competence, your skills that make you the right applicant to be hired. Well most of the candidates you are competing with, might have already put in their skills and competence.

But you have to showcase your skills that make you unique and the best of you! You have to show the interviewer that you are extremely enthusiastic to start working, and that you can create the best work environment, that other people or candidates cannot. You have to show them, how passionate you are about your work and your job. You shouldn't just say that you will do your job well, instead you should give them the assurance with specific examples, that at times of difficulties, you will be there for the firm you are working for, and can help other people do their jobs harmoniously.

When you are talking about your competence, put all your attention on your body language, since body language plays a very important role in how the person sitting in front of you perceives you. Body language is very easy to master if you follow the right steps. You have to sit upright in your chair, and your expressions must bring in a very positive atmosphere within the room and also within the mind of the hiring manager. When you are giving the answer, make sure you describe the importance of your job and also list out your previous accomplishments.

If you are a newbie, list out your accomplishments during our college term. Give examples while listing out your accomplishments. Make sure you talk about public relations and colleague relations as well.

*"I am a financial analyst with five years of work experience. In the company I am working with, I have been promoted twice within 3 years as they recognized my analytical skills. I follow the highest work ethics and have a*

*passion for analyzing data and companies. In addition, I have five years of experience with one of the best companies in industry. I think I am the best suited candidate for this position."*

## Can you work under extreme pressures?

Now, this question will determine whether you can fulfill the aspirations and expectations of the officers above you. You will have to convince the hiring manager that you will not crumble under pressure and leave the company in times of need. It is a pretty easy question if you have done your research. You can answer this question with a one word answer, but the best suggestion would be that you put your efforts in answering this question. You can answer this question using examples of time, where you raised high up the ladder when you were posed with extreme amounts of pressure. Give examples that are job and work related, do not wander around other topics, and stay up to the point. Don't stretch it too long.

For example, if an HR executive is applying for a HR manager's job, then the answer would be,

*"As an HR executive, I understand that there can be situations where I have to work under extreme pressures. However, I am known to be very patient. I can handle difficult situations with a positive attitude. For example, I had to close three senior positions in a week's time. Looking at the company's track record, it would take at least 15 days. I told my manager that I will take it as a challenge and quickly worked on filling that position very aggressively. I had to go out of my way to search and align the right candidates. I worked overtime, used all different kinds of resources and screened a lot of candidates over phone. This helped me achieve my target in six days. My manager appreciated my efforts and told me that today you have proved that you can work under pressure."*

## How do you react to changes?

Any company or firm in this world is pretty much dynamic. It can change any time and according to the situations. This question is posed to understand if you can deal well with changes, and maintain the same peaceful work atmosphere. Do not just say that you can deal with changes well. Try to backup your answer with a proper example that you can cite effectively. Again stay within the requirements of your job. Try to create such an impression, that will make the interviewer think that you aren't one of those people who are against change because they fear it, show that you don't get scared easily, and that you focus more on personal growth through change.

## What are your career ambitions and where do you see yourself in five years?

This is one of the most asked and one of the most important questions asked in any interview. By asking this question, the interviewer tends to get a brief understanding of your career goals and how the job or the company is included in the long term plan. The key to answering this question is to talk about achievable goals that are quite authentic and sound. Do not be too specific about how the job itself will meet all your career requirements or totally talk about your absurd imagination like, becoming an astronaut or buying 'Mercedes Benz' in the next five years.

A few tips you can follow while answering this question

- Keep your answers general enough so that there is no possibility of raising further questions about your job suitability.
- Express your interest in a long term-career in that position.
- Emphasize your interest in the position you are applying for as an important part of your career plan.

Example answer –

*"Currently I would like to find a role in a company, where I can hone my*

*skills and face new challenges and responsibilities overtime. My main focus would be to acquire more of the management skills in next five years, but most importantly I would extend my interest in working for a company where I can see myself getting involved in working for long-term and build my professional career."*

## Describe your perception of an ideal job.

This is something that can take a steep turn in your interview, if answered slightly wrong. You just cannot explain any ideal job. You have to explain the ideal job while tailoring it to your suitable interests. You cannot say that earning a million dollars is your ideal job. Your perception of an ideal job must sound real life, not a fantasy. Also you cannot say that your ideal job would be, you playing for your favorite football team. This can make the hiring manager think that you cannot perceive tasks properly, if put in different words or dialogues.

While answering, it would be best if you limit yourself to your job requirements and make sure that the interviewer thinks that you have sensible expectations from your job and that you are not expecting to live in some sort of dream. Concentrate more on your strengths and what you can give to the company and your job. Make sure that you convince the interviewer that you can do justice to your work. For example, let us consider a fashion designer applying for a pantaloon type retail store then the answer would be,

*"As a fashion designer, an ideal job for me would be in a place where I can explore my abilities and artistic side, while learning and gaining professional experience. Also, the job should provide me further opportunities to grow and develop myself so that I can have a strong history to support my personal and professional ambitions."*

## What makes you want to work harder?

From the perspective of the interviewer's mindset, this is a game changing question since it makes you show that you can work extremely good and can put in hard work when needed. It can be the question that is very extremely easy to answer if you are well prepared. Let us take an example of a sales executive answering this question.

*"I really enjoy working as a sales executive. Convincing a new client everyday and explaining her /him the product in detail gives me a lot of satisfaction. Moreover, I am constantly motivated by the challenge of the sale. Also, I get to interact with a lot of new people every day, which keeps me interested in the job. A challenging job which has targets and incentives makes me work hard."*

## How do your colleagues describe you?

This is another very important and sort of a tricky question that you might come across. Here, you can completely show off all your strengths and your attributes so that the hiring manager feels that you are a team player and you would do nothing that would keep the company at risk. Here, the manager shouldn't feel that you can be a risky liability to the company. Also, while showcasing your attributes, try not to come out looking arrogant or a complete show off. You have to talk about things that may represent you as a unique person in the interviewer's perception. You will have to convince your hiring manager that you are the right one for the particular position that you are applying for. Don't say stuff that may show you arrogant and over confident. Let us take an example of an international call centre executive applying for a team leader's position. The answer would be,

*"The people who work with me say that I am very friendly in nature and can easily socialize among new people. I have worked as an international call centre executive before and have successfully satisfied many customers. Due to my friendly nature and a lot of initiatives, my colleagues describe me as an employee with leadership skills."*

## What are your motivations?

It is an extremely great question, and it is a question that every interviewee must ask himself or herself before attending the interview, because it is this question that determines the seriousness of the interviewee towards the job that he or she is applying for. When giving an answer to these kinds of questions, it is recommended that your answer should have a mixture of motivations- motivations that motivate you as a person, and things that motivate you regarding your work. Again, you must be exactly to the point, and not wander to other areas of life.

And like all other questions, your answer must be tailored according to the job you are seeking. For example, do not include money as benefits or motivation unless you are applying for a sales or marketing related position, since the more you include monetary benefits, you may tend to create a wrong impression in the eyes of the hiring manager. Let us now take an example of an admin executive answering this question.

*"I am greatly motivated by meeting set targets as it provides me a feeling of satisfaction and accomplishment. I like to work hard and complete all my tasks in a given time. I feel very happy when I successfully complete my task on time or before time as I feel that my contribution can help my manager achieve targets of the department and the company."*

## What are your salary expectations and requirements?

Almost everyone works to make money for a livelihood and a lot of us want to make as much money as possible. This question is extremely tricky and you have to answer it very carefully.

*"Before attending the interview, research the market value of the job that you are applying for."*

You have to be extremely honest, when it comes to salary expectations. If you're looking for a job that will pay you a certain amount of money, but if it pays lesser than your expectations, you will soon lose interest in the job. You have to show the interviewer that you have done your research and have lots of knowledge on how much the job pays. Most people don't answer this question and create a negative impression of them. Also, do not sound desperate. Always give straight and researched answers. For example, for a position of a store manager, the answer to this question would be,

*"With 22 years of experience with one of the leading shopping malls, I am told a Store Manager at my level should be paid Rs 12 lakhs per annum, plus incentives.*

# CHAPTER 7

# Common Interview Questions

It is very important to figure out what questions can be asked in an interview.

Think about the time when your father asked to dig out all the previous year's question papers, while you were preparing for your board exams or some other important exam. Out of those too, you are asked to mark the important questions which have appeared frequently in many question papers. The case is similar with attending interviews. You need to be well prepared and to prepare well, there is no better way than to prepare the questions that are most asked in the interview.

I have prepared a list of 100 job interview questions that are generally asked in an interview. Prepare these questions to perform the best in your interview. Also, the fact remains that it is not necessary that these questions are sure to appear in any interview. Prepare as many questions as possible to easily handle the interview questions

## General Questions

- Tell me about yourself.
- Why do you want to work for this company?
- What are your greatest strengths?
- What is your greatest weakness?
- What is your greatest accomplishment?
- What drives you to achieve your goals in the workplace?
- What working environment allows you to be the most effective in your work?
- Do you work well under pressure? How?
- How do you deal with stressful situations?
- How would your work colleagues describe you?
- What are your hobbies?
- What are your workplace values?
- What is good customer service according to you?
- Why did you choose your course of study?
- If you had to describe yourself in only one word, what would it be? Why?
- Do you have any questions to ask me?
- Why do you want to leave your current job?
- Can we contact all of your references?
- Can we contact your current employer?

## Questions for Freshers

- What are your career goals and where do you see yourself in five years?
- Why should we hire you over another candidate for this position?
- Why did you apply for this position?
- Are you willing to travel/relocate for the job?
- How do you define success?
- What quality or attribute do you feel will contribute most to your career success?

- What was the most creative or innovative project you have worked on?
- What changes would you like to make if hired for this position?
- Are you currently interviewing for any other job opportunities?
- Are you willing to work for long hours and on weekends if necessary for the job?
- Describe a goal you set out for yourself in the past, and how you went about achieving it.
- If you had two job offers, what are the top five factors you would use to evaluate which is a better job opportunity?

## Questions for Middle Level Position

- Do you work best independently or as a team?
- Tell me about the time you had to sell an idea to senior management.
- What type of company culture are you looking for?
- Explain a challenge you faced in the workplace & how you solved it.
- Describe a time when you went above and beyond the normal scope of your duties.
- How would you handle having multiple tasks that need to be finished by the end of the day with no conceivable way of finishing them?
- What are you looking for in your next job?
- What are three positive things your former/current boss would say about you?
- Describe a time when your work was criticized. How did you handle it?
- How was your working relationship with your previous boss or supervisor?
- What do you expect from a supervisor?
- Can you explain the gap in your employment history?
- What would your manager say is the area you most need

development in?

- How long would you plan to stay with us, if hired?
- Tell me about a time you saved money for an employer.
- What attributes do you admire in your colleagues?
- Why have you been out of work for so long?
- Have you ever been asked to leave a position?
- Tell me about a time you had to mediate a conflict between fellow co-workers?
- Are you effective at meeting deadlines?

## Questions for Senior Level Positions

- Have you had a conflict with a colleague? How did you handle it?
- Are you more of a big-picture person or a detail-oriented one?
- Tell me about a time you disagreed with your senior about how something should be done. How did you deal with it?
- Do you feel this position would be a promotion, a lateral move, a broadening of your professional experience, or just a change? Why do you think so?
- On what position have you been most satisfied in your job?
- What is your management style?
- Why did you take a job that seems to be out of your career path?
- How do you handle constructive criticism?
- How would you establish credibility with a new team?
- Why have you changed jobs so frequently over the past few years?
- Tell us about a time your integrity was challenged. How did you handle it?
- Tell me about a time you had to give someone difficult feedback.
- What managerial task do you least enjoy?
- Have you ever written any works that have been published in a professional journal, magazine, or newspaper?
- Are you a good decision maker? Do you make decisions quickly

or do you take time to think things over before making a decision?

## Tricky and Stress Questions

- How would you describe a typical day in your current job?
- If you were an animal, which one would you want to be? Why?
- Tell me about a time that you failed at something.
- What would you do if you knew your boss was wrong about something?
- What would you do if a team member wasn't pulling his/her weight on a project?
- Do you feel you are overqualified for this position?
- What was the last book you read?
- Sell me this pen.
- What irritates you the most?
- How do you stay updated in the industry?
- If you were a tree, which kind of tree would you be?
- Our company has strong corporate social investment programs and encourages employees to participate in volunteer days. How do you feel about that? Why?
- If you find yourself getting burned out at your job, what do you do to revitalize yourself?
- What have you been doing since you were laid off?
- If a co-worker told you that he plans to call in sick for an entire week in order to take a vacation, what would you do?
- If I told you that your interview was going terribly today, what would you do?
- Is there any question I haven't asked you that I should?
- When was the last time you were angry or frustrated at work? What happened?
- What color is your brain?
- What will you do if you don't get this position?
- If you win the lottery tomorrow, would you still work?

- Do you have plans for continued study? An advanced degree?
- How do you motivate others to do their best work?
- Describe a time when you had to adapt to change. How did you handle it?
- If you could be a superhero, what power would you possess?
- In the news story of your life, what would the headline say?
- How would you fit a giraffe into a refrigerator?

I still remember hearing an incident about a young candidate who got uncomfortable to answer the questions related to his personal life and background. I don't know if it was something serious or he just couldn't share.

Many individuals attending an interview suddenly change expression when asked upon their personal life.

*"What are your hobbies and personal interests outside the work life?"*

You must be thinking, why they are so concerned about this when you have the skills that perfectly match the job or maybe you are happy about the change of topic and now you can finally talk about the cool stuff you do in your daily life.

But remember, these questions are not asked to entertain you in any manner or to make you feel proud because you can hit six in every ball of the over or how you can score a goal halfway from the football ground. Nobody is interested in your football or cricket skills, they just want to know what kind of a person are you.

Your main aim here is to convince your interviewer that you are equally talented outside the work environment and when there is a situation where you have to make a rational decision, you take the risk. You have to make the interviewer completely convinced about your skills and abilities in and out of your work environment.

Examples of the general interview questions asked in an interview.

- Are you too focused on your outside interests and hobbies?
- Do you often have many outside activities or commitments?
- How much time do you spend every day on this hobby?
- Is there any possibility that these outside commitments will distract you from your job here?
- By any chance, will we see the traces of your passion into our office?

These types of general questions can quickly get you into trouble and are asked with the same intention too. Some candidates are quite deeply involved in their hobby, while others live and drip in their hobbies. It is a fact that the more outside commitments you are involved in, the less interested your employer is in hiring you.

Now, this may sound a bit out of place since it's completely your wish what you want to do in your free time, right?

Of course, you can do whatever you want in your personal time; nobody is taking away your freedom. But there are cases where the employees get too involved in their passion and then that becomes their main focus in life, finally leaving the job.

Your employer will most probably be your well-wisher and support you in your passion too, but he also has to get the work done and run the company. He cannot search for a new candidate every time someone leaves to get hold of their passion.

## Genuine Story – About Captain Mihir

I heard about a person working in an office where my friend was his boss. His name was Mihir.

My friend would always talk about him whenever we had a conversation on phone. Mihir used to get on the nerves of his boss and I knew it through experience.

The case was that Mihir was a diehard sailor and loved sailing. He had a boat of his own which had the space for almost eight adults. It was a full-fledged serious boat that we see in movies and stunt shows.

Mihir was so much in love with his boat that he waited for weekends just like waiting for Christmas. His boat was parked at one of the beaches in Goa and his job was based in Karnataka. His family spent most of their summer living on the boat.

However, this love for boating got so serious that at one point on the weekend when the clock was at 4:59 pm, Mihir was in a ready position to race to the exit as soon as it was 5:00 pm, and when the clock struck, he raced just as expected, reached to the parking lot and drove like Fast and Furious.

The company didn't have a problem with his passion, but soon Mihir began to work sloppy. His job in the company already involved 30% travelling and every weekend this man used to travel to Goa just to sip on drinks sitting on the boat's deck and basking in sunrays.

When the records were out, Mihir was completely found out. He used the company's money for lunch and travel expenses in and out of the state. Many a times he was exhausted in the office hours because of jet lag or because he didn't get the flight and had to take other measures for reaching the office.

> *If you have too many personal commitments, the hiring manager will see this as a potential conflict in the way of work and will not hire you.*

Moreover, if you asked the man to work on extra days like Saturday, he didn't like it and it was easily visible in his attitude. And there were many cases where he showed off his love for boating, costing the company.

If you think deliberately, the efficiency of the company goes down gradually and it is too much of a risk to take. Therefore, employers these days only prefer committed, flexible and hardworking candidates in their company.

If you have too many personal commitments, the hiring manager will see this as a potential conflict in the way of work and will not hire you. This is one of the main reasons why these types of questions are commonly asked in the interview.

The best possible option to avoid this type of questions is to keep them off the resume and only mention those which are casually understandable.

# CHAPTER 8

# What to do 24 hours before the interview

I like travelling and visiting new places. So, every time I planned to visit a new place, I used to start packing my stuff 24 hours in advance. Also, before packing I used get all the stuff I need for the trip and then strike them off my list as I put them in the bag one by one. This way I used to ensure that everything I need is there and nothing else is left.

Similarly, the method holds good for an interview too. Prepare all the information, documentations, tricky questions and dress 24 hours before the interview. Once you are done with the preparation, you need to follow a schedule for the next 24 hours to ensure that you attend the interview with confidence.

Many make the mistake of leaving things to the end. The interview is at 10 in the morning, but they are still busy with ironing their dress at 9 am. Everything is put at risk like this. You need to have an actual plan of action 24 hours prior to the interview. I have prepared a 24 hour preparation plan that should be followed on the last day of preparation.

Remember, this preparation plan works best if you have been preparing for the interview way before 24 hours. If you are only preparing for 24 hours, then the preparation might not be fruitful the way you expected.

Let's assume that it is 8:00 am and you have 25 hours for your interview. For the individuals who have their interview location at an unfamiliar location, start your countdown one hour early.

## Take a Test Journey

8:00 a.m., 25 hours before the interview: Take a test journey to the interview location. Make sure to use the same means of transport that you will be using the next day that is on the interview day. If you are taking a bus or a local train, see if the same bus or train is available on the next day too. If you are driving your own vehicle, take the exact same route that you will be using the next day. You should have already figured out the location by visiting it once. This test journey is just to give you an understanding of the traffic, diversions, traffic signals or any other possible obstacles you might face while going to the location on the interview day. Also, if you are using your own vehicle, figure out where the parking is and also if it is easy to park or not.

9:00 a.m., ideally, you will have reached the place by now. Look for the parking if you have not figured it out yet. Then enter the office building to see if it is easy to find the interviewing room. If you feel that an hour is not enough to reach the venue in a safe time then make adjustments to your timings tomorrow. So, probably you should consider leaving for the interview earlier than the planned time.

While going back home, observe everything carefully to polish your visualization skills that you will use once you enter the room. Try to imagine that the interview is over and now you are going back home. Imagine that the interview was really good and spend the rest of the journey thinking about how well you performed on this important day. If any doubts are lingering in the back of your head, make sure to call the office as soon as you reach home. It won't hurt to call even if you just want to confirm the timings for one last time. You can ask about anything, maybe parking, paperwork, attire, type of interview that is going to be conducted, etc.

## Organize Outfits

10:00 a.m.: Once you reach home, arrange the outfit that you are going to wear tomorrow. Take everything out, including the belt, shoes, tie, accessories, and jewellery. Check everything carefully and ensure that your dress is clean, neat and ironed without any wrinkles. See if there is any sign of damage at all, any rips or tears, spots or missing buttons, fix them all or choose new attire. Also, make sure that your shoes are polished and shiny. Keep a plan B for your dress, just in case.

## Review All Information

11:00 a.m.: Sit on your desk and start reviewing every piece of information you have gathered till now. Obviously, this won't be the first time you are going through the data, but you need to keep them safe in your head. Go through the information you have about the organization, the industry, the interviewer and about the job itself. As you go through the content again, frame questions that can be asked related to the content. The questions may be

- What qualities you have that will make you successful in this job?
- Are you familiar with the company's history?
- Why do you want to work in our industry?
- What are the qualities that make this role serious?

## Take a Break

12:00 p.m.: Eat your lunch and relax for a while. You need good food and some peaceful time to keep your mind calm. Even in the last few hours of the interview, you need a small break so that you do not get too worked up in the last moment.

## Learn All Answers

1:00 p.m.: Break time is over, go through the questions you think you will be asked in the interview. You must have already remembered all the answers by now and you just have to go through them once. Do not try to mug up word to word answers, just read, understand and execute. Mugging up the whole answer without actually showing any emotion is of no use, the interviewer might notice that your own thoughts are not involved in the answers and you might be rejected instantly.

## Mock Interview Practice

2:00 p.m.: This is the best time to undergo a mock interview as your answers are fresh in your mind. Ask someone from your family or a friend to be the interviewer. Make it a proper dress rehearsal; ask the one taking your mock interview to evaluate all the aspects, including the dress, your response on the content and even your body language. Make sure you get everything right, the voice, the eye contact, gestures and even facial expressions.

3:00 p.m.: Take another break after the mock interview workout. Do something that you usually do to calm your mind. Do not watch anything distracting like a horror movie or a movie with too much of suspense. Watching something funny is preferable good, other things that you can do to relax is taking a hot bath, reading, yoga, bicycling, music or whatever you think is relaxing enough for you.

4:00 p.m. to 6:00 p.m.: Spend this time by taking care of your daily business like returning mails, phone calls, messages, do household chores if any, or anything else you have to do. Try not to keep your schedule with anything else that would disturb your last minute preparation later.

6:00 p.m.: Eat your dinner at this time. Fill your dinner with something nutritious and healthy, do not eat anything too heavy that can cause your stomach heavy or worse cause you indigestion. The facts say that an upset stomach can ruin your entire day and give you mood swings.

## Final Revision

7:00 p.m.: Do the final review of your information about the organization and also do a final revision of your interview questions.

8:00 p.m.: Spend time planning your interview. Imagine all the positive things that will happen in the interview and imagine that the interview is going in the right direction. Plan your actions for entry, exit and emergency situations.

## Retire

9:00 p.m. to 11:00 p.m.: Try taking your mind off the interview for a while by watching TV or playing some board game. Remember it should not be too intense like a horror movie, which can cause you nightmares or worse, a sleepless night.

11:00 p.m.: Time to sleep. You absolutely need a good night's sleep to handle the brain exercise the next morning. If you don't have the habit of sleeping early, still force yourself to sleep just in case you are nervous and you don't get sleep for a while. However, if you sleep before 11, then you just adjust the plan accordingly.

## Start Your Day

6:00 a.m.: Wake up; this should be your limit to bed. After 6, get up and brush your teeth first. Brushing will wake you up instantly and then head for a bath. Use shampoo while bathing and then use a deodorant after the bath. Avoid using cologne, which might be too intimidating for an interview. If you have a beard, shave or trim so that it looks neat and clean. It is suggested that women should wear their hair up or back so that it does not fall on their face and also put on makeup conservatively.

7:00 a.m.: Have your breakfast. Do not skip breakfast at any cost, you might not be in a mood to eat but you definitely need something to keep you strong and energetic. Also, do not wear your dress before your breakfast, accidently you might get something on it and your dress can be ruined. Drink coffee if you can't function without it.

Get dressed after you are done with your breakfast; make sure you get the dress right and perfect. Check for everything you might need at the interview like comb, breath mints, tissues, etc. Keep extra copies of your resume and examples of your portfolio as well.

8:00 a.m.: Just as you did 24 hours ago, head to the location. Try to leave a little early, analyzing the observations you made yesterday. Don't forget your phone, if anything unexpected happens on the way call the interviewer immediately and see if rescheduling is possible.

8:45 a.m.: Reach the office and head straight to the washroom for one final inspection of your dress and personality. Wipe your face with a handkerchief or a tissue. Then head to the interviewer's office and politely introduce yourself to the receptionist. Then wait for the interviewer to call in for the interview.

9:00 a.m.: Do extremely well in your interview.

10:00 a.m.: Go home while thinking about how good the interview went.

Visualizing that everything would go as smoothly as this will be an understatement. Be mentally ready for any unexpected situation and plan your way out of any obstacle. Do not panic if you cannot follow the procedure as mentioned; just adjust your time table accordingly. Your calm, collected and peaceful mind will be the key to your interview success.

# Secrets of a Successful Telephonic Interview

Earlier, phone interviews were not so popular, also the fact that there were not many candidates appearing for the interview. India was still a developing country and being educated was considered a very noble thing. However, now there are hundreds of candidates applying for one single position, resulting in a multitude of competing candidates. This became a problem for the interviewers to call every candidate and then interview them one by one to find out the right candidate. What a time consuming and brainstorming process for the interviewers!

Therefore, the best way to tackle this problem was to screen the candidates and then call the shortlisted potential ones to the interview and then pick one out of them.

The interesting fact is that now the interviewers are using telephonic interview to screen and select candidates. This solves almost all the problems of any interviewer, the interview can be conducted anytime, it is very cost effective, takes less time and is very convenient as the interviewer does not have to worry about spending an hour of his or her precious time to interview a single candidate.

Even though telephonic interview has many benefits, many companies still prefer the personal interview to select the potential candidate and use telephonic interviews as just a screening process.

> *"Even though it is a screening process, telephonic interview is very essential to get at least one step closer to getting the job."*

Few days ago, I was at a friend's place for lunch. We were just discussing about the politics and discussing how the world changed since our time, when suddenly his phone rang. He picked up and said, "Hello!" I could hear the other voice speak, "Do you have a few minutes to talk as I have made this call regarding the job application you sent."

I knew he was looking for a new job as his old job did not pay enough according to him, but he was not ready for the call now. In the middle of a lunch with a guest at home, what could be worse than that?

You can also land up in a situation like this. You might be enjoying your pizza, slouching over the couch and watching a cartoon lazily, when suddenly your phone rings and the voice says, "This is regarding the job resume you sent to our company."

You have to be prepared for a telephonic interview at all times. You might be sleeping, eating or watching a movie, the judgment call can arrive any minute. So what should you do and what should you not do while undergoing a telephonic interview?

Once you have successfully submitted the resume, you receive a message saying, "We'll call you in a few days regarding the job soon." This is the time when you should start the preparation. You already know that it is a phone interview, but you don't know when the interview will be conducted. Even if you are not specified that it will be a phone interview, your research should be able to find that out. If the job description does not mention anything about the type of interview, then it is best to ask the employer himself.



Once you are sure that you are going to face a telephonic interview, now you have to prepare. Research about the company first and make notes of everything you find. Have a copy of resume placed somewhere easily reachable, you should be able to find it instantly.

Then prepare the answers for tricky questions, behavioural questions and your responses just like you would for a personal interview. Select a place at your home, where you cannot be disturbed and there are no distractions to worry about.

Conduct mock interviews by asking someone in the family or a friend to be the interviewer. The best way to hear how you sound is to record your voice and play it. Improve wherever you feel is necessary. Prepare cheat notes and write down answers and keep them with your resume.

Understand what you need to do and what not to do during a telephonic interview.

## Telephonic Interview – Do's

- Smile, even though the hiring manager can't see you, it adds positive sense into your voice.
- Speak in a steady and calm voice. Don't rush and make sure you pronounce every word correctly. Ensure that you sound passionate and enthusiastic.
- Breathe normally. I know it is a nervous situation but you need to

breathe normally and stay calm. Breathing will help you relax and answer questions easily.

- Listen to the questions carefully. Do not hurry and give the answer which you feel is right. Give them the answers they need.
- Keep the glass of water nearby. The situation can become complex with a dry mouth.
- Address the name of the interviewer in an appropriate manner. It's your employer on the phone and not your college mate.
- Take your time and answer the questions once you collect all the thoughts. It is your time to shine, do not be nervous.
- Keep your cheat notes close. If there are any technical questions asked, you should be able to answer them confidently.
- Ask relevant questions at the end of the interview. Also, confirm what the next step is and when can you hear from the company again.

## Telephonic Interview – Don'ts

- Do not eat anything during the telephonic interview. No matter how hungry you are it's just a matter of 10-15 minutes, hold your hunger.
- Do not smoke at any cost. Smoking can leave you often taking a pause in the conversation, which can leave the interviewer wondering if you are actually focused or not.

- Never ever interrupt the interviewer when he/she is speaking. Nothing is more irritating then cutting someone off in the middle while speaking.
- Do not answer the questions with just a "yes" or "no". Elaborate your answers and explain why it is "yes" or "no". Provide relevant examples wherever you can.
- Don't be too casual and keep your language professional. Avoid using any type of slang or a short form.
- Avoid giving long winded answers to the questions asked. Keep your answers to the point.

So now you are completely prepared for the telephonic interview. When the phone rings and you are asked for a few minutes, politely respond that you are ready for the interview. Quickly grab a glass of water, notepad and pen, your notes and resume and head to the selected location at your home.

The hiring manager will not call you to the personal interview until and unless he is interested in you, your skills and abilities, knowledge and accomplishments. Be confident while speaking and answer every question with a bold attitude.

## 7 Phone Interview Tips to a Fabulous Phone Interview

*Phone Interview Tip 1: Request the Specific Time Most Suitable For You*

Its very nerve breaking and irritating to be waiting for an interview call that can ring up anytime you are least expecting. Your nervousness reaches the hype and you can't wait still. In the meantime if you get the call, you are already frightened to death. Obviously, you are in no position to attend the call.

You've already had a very rough day till now and the last thing that could make it worse is a call asking for your interview at the time when you are least prepared. It's really sound when you ask the person interviewing you to call at a specific time. In this way you are ready when the call arrives, get over with it and then you can turn towards other activities of life.

You cannot just continue your interview when you are not ready thinking that it is completely unreasonable to ask the interviewer to call later. The interviewer understands that you have things to do in your life and you may be caught up doing any one of those. It's okay to reschedule your phone interview.

All you have to say is, "Thank you so much for calling, however, I will be at my best at 4:30 / second half today. Will you be free to interview me then, please?"

If in any case, the HR manager refuses, just gulp it down and face the interview. There has to be a good reason why the HR manager cannot adjust to your timings.

But, the major point to understand here is that, the more control you have over the interview, the better it is.

Try as much as you can to get a time fixed for the interview. If you can figure out when the interview will start, then you can pre-arrange your mindset for the interview by then and you will be in your best shape to answer the call.

There are many cases where the interviewers were too impressed by the candidate's character that he was offered the job after interviewing him for 10 minutes on phone. The man who won the job had asked the interviewer at the time of his application specific timings during the day when he was available for the interview. This way the candidate knew when the call would arrive.

*Phone Interview Tip 2: Be Ready to Face the Phone Interview*

The important benefit of the phone interview is that the interviewee can have the access to all the notes and critical points.

Put your notes in front of you when the phone call arrives, but make sure not to read them. Remember, the best thing to prepare for a phone interview is to read out the answers aloud. If you throw out words like a parrot, the interviewer will notice it very soon.

You cannot be caught cheating on a phone interview, until and unless you want them to catch you. Keep your natural speaking tone while you give your answers.

Select a quiet place for the interview, where you cannot be disturbed. Inform your family about the important phone call firsthand and let them not disturb you. If you have a dog, then make sure you have it put away so that if it barks, the sound does not reach you.

I've conducted many phone interviews myself and believe me when I say that I speak from experience, it's very annoying when you are in the middle of an important question and someone asks you, what you're going to have for lunch.

It is very important to keep a good attitude during the entire phone interview. The interviewer is assessing you every moment. Even the slightest mistake can change their opinion for you.

*Phone Interview Tip 3: Remove your Caller Tune*

It's very common these days that the caller tunes are activated so that any person who calls can enjoy the music till it is answered.

Trust me, it is extremely unprofessional to have a caller tune when you are about to get an important phone interview call. The interviewer is not at all interested in your music interests.

Strictly deactivate any caller tune to maintain a calm and professional understanding between you and the interviewer.

I once called a candidate for a phone interview and I was entertained with a very popular Bollywood item song. Nice song, but you don't want your future boss to hear these songs when they call you. It is too risky, just change it.

*Phone Interview Tip 4:Don't Answer any Other Calls during the Interview*

*Never, ever do this!*

If you can disable the function on your phone, excellent, but if you answer any other call during the interview, then you send out the wrong message that the phone interview is not very important to you.

You can just ignore the calls or reject them for a few minutes if you have to. Every other thing can wait; the phone interview is the most important matter in hand.

*Phone Interview Tip 5: Do not be Afraid to Ask about the Interview*

When you are at the end of the interview, do not just bluntly say "Goodbye" or "Thank-you for the interview", give your interviewer a few options to when you are available for the actual meeting.

This breaks the ice between you and the interviewer about the important facts and also, makes it easier for them to plan their timings. Moreover, it is an excellent opportunity to get their review on how the interview was perceived.

It is a good sign if they tell you that they will discuss and notice you later or if they give you any other dates they are available on. It indicates that you performed well in the interview and you will most likely score the interview.

If you don't ask the facts then you will be back to square one, waiting for their call all day long and getting disappointed if the call doesn't arrive on that day. Make sure you are taking this somewhere.

*Phone Interview Tip 6: Be Yourself*

Communication experts have reported that 80% of our communication to one another is non-verbal.

It is extremely difficult to understand someone by just hearing their voice on the phone. Make sure you are constantly smiling and giving indications that you are properly listening to each and every word the interviewer is speaking.

> *"Facts say that the number one reason for people to be rejected over phone is due to lack of enthusiasm."*

You have to project a very positive and enthusiastic image, convincing the interviewer that you have confidence and potential.

Avoid eating, drinking anything or chew gum. I am not asking to ground yourself, just be you, but do not project an image of a completely relaxed candidate who is enjoying his life too much.

Facts say that the number one reason for the applicants to be rejected over the phone is due to lack of enthusiasm. The second reason is, extremely poor communication skills; some talk too much, some too less, while some talk in a monotonous voice throughout the interview.

*Phone Interview Tip 7: Expect Gaps during Your Phone Interview*

Your interviewer will be most likely writing down notes as you give your answers. Their hands are busy while they are talking to you and your each and every important response goes in there.

Some interviewers are too busy writing notes that they forget to give a proper feedback. Normally in a personal interview, you would receive a response immediately after your response, an occasional smile or a nod. Anything done after hearing your answer is a feedback.

They might be nodding their head or smiling and since you can't see him, you don't know if he gave you a feedback or not. Do not be agitated to hear a response by asking if he was hearing or not. This can make you nervous. Expect possible gaps and after you are finished, if the interviewer couldn't hear you, he or she will ask you to repeat it.

## Common Phone Interview Questions and Answers

*Tell us something about yourself.*

You must be thinking, why God, why! But yes that's the truth; this question is a very frequent opening question to your interview innings. For inexperienced candidates this question can be a major setback if they don't understand how to answer this question. Just talk about your important qualifications and the certificates which are specifically related to the job interview. Tell the interviewer about how you have prepared to be a potential candidate for the role.

*What type of job opportunity are you expecting?*

This question is commonly asked to those candidates who have not mentioned any specific role in their resume. Often this question is asked by the interviewer to know if the candidate is actually interested in the role they are offering or just looking for any job opportunity. For starters, you definitely should mention in your resume what role you are opting for. It makes things very easy and smooth.

However, if you have not mentioned in your resume because you don't have any proper idea about the post available, you can always ask the interviewer to share some details about the role(s) available. After hearing about what actually you have to do in the job, you can decide whether you are interested in it or not. If you are not interested, then it is better to back down early as you don't want to invest too much of time in something that won't help you on the long run.

*Will you be able to relocate?*

Indeed, a difficult question it is. Many interviewers like to confirm firsthand before proceeding with the job interview if you can change your location to where the job is based. If you have not thought about relocation, then you better think about it now. You can be left thinking when you are asked this question, making the interviewer wait and giving him hints that you are unsure about your decisions. Another tip for starters, if you are ready to relocate, mention it in your resume. The more details you provide, the better it is to find the job you want.

For bigger employers, there may be multiple locations. Moreover this is not about what you consider as an ideal location, but it is about what you would and would not consider as potential locations according to you, so take it seriously.

*What is your expected salary range?*

This is a common question among the experienced hires conducted by large corporates; however, it can occur during the entry level and internship hires conducted by big companies too. The interview concludes two things with this question, first is whether you are available within their expected salary range and the second is that if you are actually worth the money spent.

If you are unsure of how to reply then simply ask what the offered salary range for the job is. If the salary range is within your expected range, then you sign the agreement.

*Share an example of __________.*

This is obviously the standard behavioural question in the interview. You can expect many of these during the course of the interview. Answer this using the STAR approach mentioned before. Using the STAR method is the best way to answer this question; you can give a good answer in this way even if you have not been asked any behavioural question before.

"Let me give you an example...." Or "Thank-you for the question...." are great follow ups to boost your answer in any behavioural question.

*Can you please share some more details about__________?*

This is one of the typical interview questions where the interviewer would like to know more details about something that is of interest in your resume. It could be anything, any certificate course or an internship you attended during your summer break. Just answer properly using examples, if any and you will be able to get through it.

*What else do you know about _________?*

This question can strike you in many formats. It is specifically a technical question and there are many ways to answer this too. These types of questions are asked to assess your skills and knowledge regarding the role you are going to play in the company if you are selected. It could be about a tool if you are into mechanical business field or about a software or computer language, if you are into the IT and software industry. Also, finish the question with a behavioural example, it creates a good impression.

**CHAPTER 10**

# 10 Job Interview Blunders and How to Avoid Them

E veryone talks about what to do during an interview, but it is also very important to know what not do in an interview. There have been many occasions in my life, when I faced candidates who do disturbing things in an interview like picking their nose or scratching their heads constantly. It is important to understand that even simple things that you do can take you miles away from the job that can be yours.

*"In a poll, interviewers were asked to name the most common blunders that candidates make during an interview. Almost 51% of the hiring managers talked about dressing inappropriately, while 49% stated that bad mouthing a former boss was at hype too. Apart from these, 48% pointed out that the candidates were not interested, 44% told that they were arrogant, 30% stated that the*

If you sum up the blunders above, they just make a whole list of things that should be strictly avoided in an interview. You are going to attend an interview for a job that can set your life on the right path, how can you neglect the crucial points that tell you about the things that should be absolutely avoided. After interviewing thousands of candidates and training millions of professionals, I have brought you a list of common mistakes candidates do, which you should understand and avoid doing.

*You are going to attend an interview for a job that can set your life on the right path, how can you neglect the crucial points that tell you about the things that should be absolutely avoided.*

**Arriving Late:** which is the mistake that some of the candidates commit. Even if the traffic was too much to handle or your bike suddenly stopped at nowhere, you absolutely cannot risk getting late. Make sure you know the location two or three days prior to the interview. Calculate how much time it takes to reach the location and leave an extra half-hour early just in case your bike stops or there is too much of traffic.

*Prashant Shetty appeared for a Physical Trainers job in an international school at 10.45 am in place of 10 am. He did not clear that interview and the primary reason could have been late arrival.*

**Lack of preparation** is one of the biggest mistakes that candidates make. If you take the job interviews lightly, then the interviewers take you just as lightly. Remember, interview is an examination that you need to pass with excellent grades and you have to prepare for an interview just as you would for an exam. Make sure you try your level best to figure out what type of an interview it is going to be and how will the interview go about. By knowing more about the interview that you are going to attend, will give you a huge advantage while preparing for that interview. If you are not able to answer the basic questions related to the job, it creates an impression that you are not serious about getting the job and it can reduce your chances of getting hired immediately.

*Krupa Asher appeared for an interview for the post of Senior Accountant. She had 12 years of experience and was not aware that it will be a technical interview. The interviewer was Finance Head and he asked some basic questions about most popular accounting software and she could not answer as she was not prepared. She lost one big opportunity due to lack of preparation.*

**Dressing inappropriately** also deducts your points in an interview. The first thing the interviewers will notice after you enter the room is your dress and creating a positive first impression can lead to a smooth interview ahead. Also, make sure you dress according to the job you are applying for. If you are applying for a casual job like waiting tables, the dress you will wear for that interview will be different than the dress you will wear while attending an interview for a managerial position.

> ***"Although, dressing good for an interview will not get you the job, but if you ignore the dressing, the chances are that you will lose the job."***

**Badmouthing**, as mentioned before was the reason for 49% of the interviewers rejecting the candidates. This includes badmouthing anyone from your previous job or a current one; let it be an employee, boss, or a receptionist. Nobody would like to hire a person who complains behind the back and it also creates a negative impression of your personality. Absolutely avoid badmouthing and I cannot stress this enough, but be positive at all times.

**The key to success is
to know whom to blame
for your failure.**

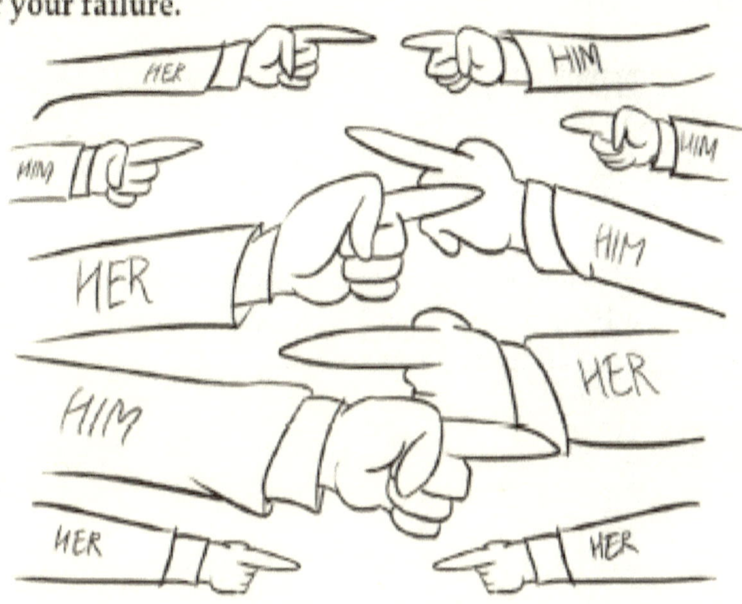


**Bad body language** like mumbling, using slang in every sentence or crossing your arms during an interview can land you directly out of the interview. Your body language is extremely important and is constantly being noticed by the hiring managers. Avoid being rigid or slouching, hide your nervous gestures as much as possible and do not use too much of your hands when talking.

**Never be rude or abusive.** You must be rolling your eyes stating that you already know this one. However, you never know what situation your interviewer will put you in and you end up being angry and land up in a situation you would not like to. Keep calm and be patient, this is just a test that you are going through and will have no effects on your real life. Losing your temper in the middle of an interview, becoming total defensive and using abusive language are the best ways to not get hired, once the damage is done you cannot fix it.

*Minal Rungta was being interviewed for the post of an English Teacher. She was asked to share the most difficult time she had with the current employer. As the interviewer asked a lot of questions, she started to lose temper and hence lost the job opportunity.*

**Poor communication skills** are the major reason for a lot of candidates not getting hired. Unless and until your communication skills are improved, you cannot explain what you want to express in the best way possible. Most of the candidates who cannot communicate effectively try to answer questions in a simple "yes" or "no", you have to remember that a yes or no will not be enough to satisfy the HR manager. Engage with your interviewer and let him know that you are an excellent candidate for the post.

**Talking too much** can take away the job opportunity just as using an abusive language. In an interview, nobody is interested in what you did your entire life, your experiences, learning, and wisdom, just answer the question that has been asked. Keep your answers short, to-the point and completely focused on the topic. No trash talking.

*"The best way to answer the questions is to keep it simple and be honest about what is asked by the interviewer."*

**Not answering the question** might be an easy way to skip the difficult situation you are facing, but this creates an impression that you were not prepared enough for the interview. It is extremely frustrating for an interviewer to ask a question and then get a blank stare. The interviewer needs an answer and you have to give him a straight answer, no matter what. Make sure you understand the question well before finally giving your answer.

**Not following up** after the interview, no matter how good the interview was, it can create a bad impression on the interviewers. If you have not received any notice from the interviewer within a few days, do not hesitate to call back and reiterate your interest in the job. Also, send a follow up thank-you letter or an email to leave a good lasting impression.

These are the common interview blunders that candidates make; make sure you avoid them during your interview. Apart from these common mistakes, a candidate can make bigger mistakes too, like submitting the wrong resume or saying something by mistake that should have not been said. In these circumstances, if you recover the mistake effectively then there are still a few chances left to create a good impression on the interviewer.

## Major Interview Mistakes and How to Recover Them

No matter how thoroughly you prepare for an interview, mistakes can still happen. What matters here is will you be able to recover after making the mistake or due to extreme tension you will step back. Just think about a situation where you have worked hard to get an opportunity working in your dream company. You finally get an interview, where you absolutely have to shine. You have prepared good enough to answer all the tricky questions and situations that will be asked in the interview. On the day of interview, you are completely prepared and just when you think that nothing could go wrong you see an error in your resume that is completely avoidable. You miss the bus and now you are very late for the interview or some other mistake that should not have happened. In this case, you cannot back down from your dream job, can you? You have to move forward, always, plus you should cover up the mistakes effectively. I have compiled a few major mistakes that could be committed by any candidate along with the possible recovery options.

*Submitting the Wrong Resume*

It is a good option to have different versions of your resume for different jobs you are applying for, but that does not mean you have one resume for every job you are applying for. What if you send out one of the resume that was meant for a different job?

Now, if the resume you submitted had small variations from the one that you actually had to send, then let it go. But if it was completely different, let's say you are applying for a marketing position and your resume focuses completely on corporate communications; try to recover it by sending an apology letter or a mail as soon as possible. State that the resume you previously submitted was not the best one and attach the correct resume.

If you still get the interview even with the wrong resume, then send the correct resume to the hiring manager prior to the interview and also distribute the hard copies of resume to the hiring managers once you have entered the room. Do not point out the mistakes in front of them, simply cover it up by saying, "This is my most relevant and up-to date resume." Being paranoid about sending the wrong resume will not solve the problem, covering up with quick actions surely will.

## Mixed up appointment

If you really want a job and you have sent countless resumes to many different companies, then your calendar will surely be full of interviews. That is actually good, until there are two interviews on a single date, or worse you misunderstood the meaning for, "next Monday".

There is nothing you can do in this situation except calling as soon as possible after you realized the mistake. Do not give a long sorry explanation, which they are not interested in. Just tell them about your calendar dates mixing up and you regret it deeply and then ask them if the interview can be rescheduled anytime the hiring manger is free.

One of my friends once landed in this situation. He arrived at the wrong office at the right time by mistake. He told me that a quick phone call and an apology helped him sort out the situation. Also, he followed it up by a short message expressing his sincere interest in the position.

Getting your mistakes right and making a practical effort to connect with the interviewers is exactly what they want from a candidate. Following up in this way might give you a second chance to prove your worthiness.

## Arriving Late at the Interview

It may be your fault or not, arriving late at an interview always creates a bad impression on the hiring managers. Therefore, if your car broke down, or if you missed the local train, or even if you slightly feel that you are going to be late for the interview, call up the manager and inform about your position. Letting the manager be aware of your current situation and apologizing before you actually get late is a better option than letting the hiring manager sitting in the chairs and waiting for you.

> *"Remember there is just one chance for making the first impression; you don't want your first impression to be an unpleasant."*

Always remember not to make lame excuses for being late. Make a call and apologize for being late.

*Stammering while you answer the question*

There is a perfect answer in your mind for every question that the interviewer asks and you execute them flawlessly until you are asked a difficult one. You know the answer, but you are nervous and while you are speaking you stammer from time to time.

Do not be paranoid, just calm down, everyone makes these mistakes and it's better to pause and collect your thoughts instead of continuing to stammer every word. The interviewer knows it is a difficult question and he understands the reason behind your stammering. So, if you are making a lot of blunders while answering, do not worry too much and start sweating, just take a deep breath and rephrase your answer.

Instead of focusing on what you could have done later, just think about how you can add a positive effect on it.

> *"You have to understand that the most important aspect of coming back from a blunder is to keep your cool; it is more likely that the interviewer will be impressed by your recovery instead of the continued stammering answer."*

# Common Spelling Mistakes Made by a Lot of Candidates

I was teaching a few students recently, when I noticed a simple mistake on one of the student's answers. He wrote "freinds" instead of writing "friends". When I corrected him, he casually replied that it is a very minor mistake and can be neglected. Since, I have the eyes and mind of an interviewer; I couldn't simply let it go and made him write the correct spelling ten times so that he could learn.

Similarly, there are many spelling mistakes that a candidate makes in his resume or while writing a screening test. Spelling mistakes could be just a minor error, but since English is a tricky language, change of characters can lead to an entirely different meaning. There are many words which have different spellings, but have the same pronunciation and nobody cares to correct them. However, nothing could be avoided from the interviewer's eyes and he evaluates each and every single mistake you make. These minor errors may not be much, but may become the reason for the next candidate to land up with the job since he has the spellings right. I researched and found out few words that could confuse your senses. This confusion between the words may make a large difference in your resume.

### Adverse and Averse

Here, the word *adverse* means harmful or unfavorable, while the word *averse* means dislike or opposition. The word adverse could be used like "Adverse market conditions were the reason for poor sale" and averse could be used like "I was averse to paying Rs 1000 a share for a company that generates no revenue."

### Affect and Effect

The usage of this set of words could be tricky. The words *affect* means to have an influence on something, while the word *effect* means to accomplish something. For affect, you can take the example of "Your work has a critical affect on the company's revenues." When it comes to effect, you can take the example of "The board effected a sweeping policy change."

Use the word effect when something is implemented and use affect when you are having an impact on something.

## Compliment and Complement

*Compliment,* obviously means to say something nice to someone or maybe praise someone or something, on the other hand, *complement* means to add, improve, enhance, complete or bring close to perfection. *So, I can compliment your dressing style, but you still have to complement your skills and qualifications.*

## Criteria and Criterion

Here, the tricky thing is that the *"criteria"* is plural, while the *"criterion"* is singular. You can normally use the words such as "reasons" or "factors" to avoid confusion between these words.

## Discreet and Discrete

"We made discreet inquiries to determine if the landlord was willing to sell the apartment." Here *discreet* means being careful, cautious or showing good sense of judgment.

"We analyzed data from different a number of discrete websites to determine the actual price of the object." Here *discrete* means individual, separate or distinct.

## Insure and Ensure

This one is easy to understand. *Insure* means like an insurance, whereas *ensure* means to make sure. You can get something valuable insured or you can ensure that it is kept safe.

## Principal and Principle

I am surprised that candidates still get these words wrong. This was explained since school time by your English teacher when you wrote "To the Principle" instead of "To the Principal" in your leave letter or maybe an apology letter.

A *principle* is a fundamental and a *principal* refers to primary or first preference.

## It's and Its

*It's* is the short form or a contraction of it is, while *its* can be referred to someone or something. For an example, "it's collar is blue" is wrong, while "its collar is red" is right. The best way to solve this confusion is to simply extract the word it's into it is and then see how the sentence sounds. For an example you can write "it's hot" like "it is hot".

## They're and Their

This is the same case as the previous one. *They're* is the contraction of "they are" and *their* refers to someone's property. So the next time you are confused, just split the word and you will understand. For example, "they're late" can be written as "they are late".

## You're and Your

One more of the apostrophes, *"you're"* is also a contraction of "you are" and everyone knows the meaning of *"your"*. Just connect the dots and you will be able to understand the sentence.

# Recovering from an Interview Disaster

Let's just pretend that even after you did everything right, followed all the guidelines, was not late for the interview, answered all the questions confidently, but still could not win the job. Why? You must have made a mistake that you did not notice then, but you realized it as soon as you walked out of the door, it could be something that you forgot to mention in your resume, or maybe a key point that you forgot to mention in an answer, which was crucial for your selection.

So how do you actually recover from a blow that hard? You wouldn't want to waste all that preparation you did for that interview, that perfect resume you build cannot be thrown into the trash, the techniques you mastered should not be lost and the opportunity should not be ignored.

It could be a tricky process to make the wrongs right after you walked out. In any case, if you still want to take the initiative to make one final attempt, you need follow these four steps to make sure that you are brave enough to meet face to face with your blunders.

### Step 1 - Do not Over Analyze

It's obvious that you will be replaying the entire interview in the back of your head at the time of final handshake. You analyze each and every part of the interview to see if there was something left out or something that you did wrong. In your head you will be remembering: Did you smile? Did you ask the right questions? Did you convince the hiring managers that you are a potential candidate?

The more you think about the interview, the more details will ring your head. Then small mistakes will start troubling you, for example, you may start getting worried about the part where you stammered while answering about your weakness or you were not too confident about your future plans.

In most cases, these small mistakes won't damage a lot. These are just the minor slip-ups that happen with every candidate and also, the interviewer understands them. Moreover, it is considered best not to bring these tiny mistakes up again, which will be more like going to your teacher and getting your numbers detected because you wrote a wrong answer.

However, if you still think that there was a major blunder made, like not attaching an important document with your resume or something similar, then you have to proceed to the step two, where you figure out what to do next.

### Step 2 – Figure out your next action

To tell the truth, post-interview damage control can be very risky. Some hiring managers might see it in a positive way, while for others it would be just bringing up a mistake that they failed to notice. Therefore, it is extremely important to find out the errors specifically, which are important enough to bring up again and if bringing them will actually help you. You need to ask a couple of questions to find out if the mistakes were worth the damage control.

### Was it a Make-or-Break mistake?

Firstly, it is quite important to understand if the mistake you made had any impact on the interview at all. Maybe while answering a question, you forgot to mention one of the important points; this may not affect the interviewer's decision much if the final answer was fairly acceptable.

However, if you are attending an interview out of town and you forgot to mention the point that you are perfectly fine with relocating or maybe your experience was in question and you did not mention an internship you did in that field, then in these cases damage control can be worth the risk.

### Can you recover by sharing addition info?

One of the important factors of damage control is being able to recover your mistake in a concise manner. If there is a possibility to provide additional information in a few short sentences, then you can proceed with the plan, but in case your recovery includes lengthy pages and a sorry explanation, the interviewer might be disappointed. No hiring manager would be interested to spend time reading your long explanations when they had just taken out time to meet you personally.

Also, it is considered better to let it go if your recovery sounds more like an apology instead of providing some new information. The point to remember here is that if you are not providing any new information as a candidate, then it is simply best to put the matter at rest.

If after considering both the questions, you are still left with a vital piece of information to share that is absolutely essential, then you can proceed with the damage control action, however, if there is no extra piece of information to add and you still dig in with a sorry face, it is more likely to create a negative impression than expecting a good one.

*Step 3 – Fix it gracefully*

The best way to approach the blunder you made in the interview is through a short and simple note. You can simply send a mail with merely two paragraphs, giving not much room for explanation. I repeat; until and unless it is extremely important to do the damage control, do not proceed with the plan of action.

You can just add a casual note, which includes a small sorry and a request to consider the information that you want to add. Do not expand the note aimlessly and keep it as short as possible. The interviewer is not going to give you points for your writing, especially when you had made a mistake and want to do the damage control.

*Step 4- Learn from it*

The most important damage control one can do is to learn from the blunder you did and prepare for the next one effectively. Think about the reasons that lead to the mistake, think about the reason for why you were nervous at the last moment and you started biting your lips.

Try to conduct as many mock practices as possible to perform better. Ask someone from your friends or family to rate your confidence and to pinpoint where you are going wrong. Try to perform in front of an audience, like your family or friends. The more comfortable you will be while answering a question, the more confident you will be in the real interview.

List out the blunders you made and make sure that you do not do them in any other interview.

It is always very difficult to accept the fact that you made a mistake that you shouldn't have done, but before you jump in to save yourself, it is probably better to realize that they are not as bad as you think. Moreover, if you are the right fit for the job, the interviewer will definitely know.

# CHAPTER 11

# Interview Success Stories to Learn From

We all know that clearing an interview is not an easy job. One has to study, research, analyze, practice and do much more to finally gain the result one has been hoping for. In these hard working times, taking a look at those scenarios where people have successfully completed the milestone that you are planning to do yourself, will motivate you and give you a clear idea about how to execute your own plans.

Reading interview success stories has always helped the young aspirants and those who have unfortunately failed a few times. It will help in understanding the concept and find out what mistake they are making.

Every story has its own plot and its own reason for inspiring others. Reading these stories and understanding the moral in them is extremely important to have a positive impact. I have compiled a few stories, which I felt would be the most helpful stories for you.

# An Intelligent IT Professional

*The first story that I would like to include in this list is about an IT professional Devanand Chaoudhary. Devanand is fresher applying for a job in large Software Development Company and I am very thankful to him for posting this story online. I was going through some technical stuff when I stumbled upon this story.*

*The interviewer interviewing Devanand was quite frank and always noticed things to complete detail. Devanand had presented an excellent CV which almost gave all the academic insights clearly to the interviewer. The interviewer was quite pleased to see such a good CV.*

*Since, the CV gave all the academic insights, the interviewer focused mainly on the psychological aspects. Most of the questions that were asked were*

aimed at judging the candidate's personality and character. Few questions that were asked are given below

- *Do you notice anything unnecessary in this room?*
- *What changes would you like to make in this room?*
- *Would you still work with us if you were given a high post but a low salary?*

Devanand tackled all the questions very intelligently. He gave honest answers to every question, pointed out a few things that he thought were out of place, like the water filter should have been kept near the door and the extra lights which were not needed in the room. He also pointed out the symmetry of the chairs and that the phone was kept at a wrong place.

When the salary question was asked, he cleared to the interviewer that he was more interested in learning and gaining experience rather than focusing on money. Devanand nailed the interview and was offered various positions in the company, having the choice of choosing any one he liked.

The key things that made Devanand so preferable in this interview were the easy and proper layout of his CV, which clearly explained his academic qualifications and practical experience, the confidence with which he expressed his views, the honest answers that he gave to every question asked and also the determination to learn and grow.

## Smart Receptionist

The second story that I would like to share is about the interview conducted for the position of a receptionist. Sushma Singh Rajput was the candidate here and the interviewer was a very strict and self made man. It was a three star hotel where the receptionist was needed.

Sushma was a very strong woman and always acted according to the situation. Her analyzing skills were on par, which was the main reason to impress such a strict interviewer. She was a beginner and didn't have much experience, which actually irritated the interviewer who expressed that he *wasn't quite interested in giving the position to a beginner.*

*However, Sushma didn't hesitate and expressed her dedication and interest in the job. The interviewer tried to put her away by asking her many tricky questions for which Sushma replied extremely well. Few questions that were asked are*

- *How would you manage an angry customer?*
- *This is a repetitive job, what will keep you motivated to do well every day?*
- *If a customer accused you for bad service, what would you do?*

*Sushma understood that the interviewer wanted to put her away, but she didn't give up. She gave all the answers with utmost confidence. For angry customers, she said that she will offer a glass of water and ask the customer to calm down till the problem is solved. If the customer still does not bring down the heat, she said that she will call the manager instantly.*

*When it comes to motivation, she instantly said that she liked the job of being a receptionist as it allows her to interact with many different people. She also mentioned that the job is repetitive, but the excitement of meeting new people everyday will keep her motivated to perform well.*

*Finally, when she was asked about being accused of bad service, she confidently said that she would immediately apologize to the customer for bad service and ask for an immediate feedback so that she could correct the mistake next time.*

*The sheer confidence and positive answers given by Sushma impressed the strict interviewer and she was instantly hired for the job.*

## A Real Accountant

*Adding to the list is the interview conducted for the position of an accountant. Our candidate Rajesh Mishra was asked the five most common questions that are asked for a job of an accountant, they are:*

- *What is your reason to become an accountant?*
- *What knowledge do you possess regarding accounting standards?*
- *In what ways can you minimize your work errors?*
- *Tell us about a time when you helped in reducing costs?*
- *Where do you see yourself in five years?*

*That's right, these are the five questions he was asked to answer. Rajesh was not much experienced, but he was good in what he did. He had prepared for these questions well and answered them to full stop.*

*He said, he chose accounting as a career because since childhood he was good at numbers and could do complex calculations with ease. Moreover, he had completed the certification course of the most popular accounting software. Regarding accounting standards, he spoke confidently about the existing tax norms and the latest developments relevant to the business of the company he was applying for.*

*He said he can minimize his work errors by increasing his speed of typing, learning from seniors and also shared that he had the habit of checking the work while doing data entry which drastically reduces the chances of errors.*

*It was a typical interview where the confidence and hard work is counted. You may not be an extraordinary candidate and neither Rajesh was. He just worked hard and prepared for what was coming. He was offered the job in the company along with a decent salary.*

*The main point of including this story is because this is a standard example of a successful interview. Rajesh's hard work and dedication earned the post, which all the aspiring candidates wish for.*

## Deserving Team Leader – Internal Promotion Interview

*I would like to mention one more interview which has a lot to learn from. An interview was conducted within the firm to select a team leader for an important upcoming project.*

*Total fifteen employees were invited for the interview and a bonus was promised for the employee who gets selected. Just like other fourteen employees, Vaibhav Tyagi was also invited. Among the fourteen employees, the uncommon thing about Vaibhav was that he was working in the firm since two years, while the other candidates were part of the firm since very long.*

*When the interview began, it was divided into three parts, an aptitude test, group discussion and personal interview. To everyone's surprise, Vaibhav scored the highest in the aptitude test and spoke extremely well in group discussion. Also, not only he let the others speak, but also gave more priority to the members who were very senior to him.*

*When he was called for the personal interview, he was asked, "So, Mr. Tyagi, why do you think you are better than other fourteen candidates?" to which he simply replied, "I really cannot compare myself to the others when it comes to experience, but I am sure that if the opportunity is given, I can prove that I am much faster and well organized. I think that every member in the team is equally important and has a unique role to play. My first thing, if selected as a team leader, would be to find out the specialties of my team mates and assign them work in which they are best. Even after becoming a team leader, I think that proper respects should be given to all those candidates who deserve it."*

*With excellent performance in all three rounds, without a doubt he was assigned the team leader's position. Later the project was a complete success and promoted Vaibhav for his extraordinary way of working. The key things that separated Vaibhav from the other invitations were that he was very well organized and took interest in what he did. He respected his seniors and gave everyone equal space to grow. He was friendly with everyone. His team members were extremely happy working under such a talented team leader, even the senior employees in the team appreciated his work.*

*Most of the employees who did not qualify for the post, complained about giving him the opportunity of leading a project as a team leader since Vaibhav was not much experienced.*

## Becoming a Sales Executive

Another example that I would like to share with you is about the position of a corporate sales executive. It is often said that it is a tough job to be a corporate sales executive and therefore, the interviews conducted are also equally tough.

Hiring Mangers hope to hire someone who has good speaking skills, who is very confident and target oriented. This is because, corporate sales executives are an important link to the clients and only the best are chosen for this matter.

One such candidate Rishab Sharma was very keen to become a corporate sales executive for a professional software company. His level of dedication was very high and he had prepared in every manner he could before stepping into the interview room. His resume was properly organized and highlighted his key achievements and goals. His dressing and grooming was perfect for the corporate sales executive's job and his body language displayed that he was very confident.

When the interview started, he managed to get a good start. He was prepared for all the questions and was answering them with his best positive note, until he was caught off guard. His right leg was shaking and he didn't notice it. The hiring managers saw what was happening and threw a direct question at him, "Why is your leg shaking so much, are you nervous?"

Rishab just looked at his leg shaking and realized that he suddenly was very nervous. He could almost feel the job slipping from his hands. He had to give a positive response even in that situation, if not, all the hard work he had done would have been wasted. He calmed down and collected his thoughts and replied in his utmost confident tone, "I am very sorry for this interruption, it was always my goal to work as a corporate sales executive in a professional company as yours and I have worked very hard for it. I have to admit that I am a bit nervous because this corporate sales executive job in your company is very important for me. I want this job in order to prove that I can achieve targets and prove my abilities. I have prepared well for this interview and I am very dedicated about working in this firm."

*Pulling out a professional yet positive answer in a situation like this is a great come back. Upon receiving the above response, the hiring manager was dearly impressed and offered him corporate sales position in that interview.*

*The key points that need to be drawn from the above instance is that you may be nervous in an interview, but it is natural. Accepting the truth and using the situation to your advantage is the best way to get out of the situation. People normally think about the damage done, but the secret is to think about how to recover the damage already done, instead of panicking.*

# CHAPTER 12

# How to Follow up After the Interview

## Follow the right steps to secure your job

So after your ideal job interview, you get some information from the interviewer about your performance and what to expect next. But, what if, you never ask or forget to ask out of nervousness or the interviewer puts you off and leaves you in a maze? The next best idea in your mind is to simply call them and ask but, what if, they tell you to wait and you still don't hear from them for a while? Finally, you conclude that they might not be interested in hiring you.

What now? Would you surrender?

Or

Would you think outside the box?

Find the interviewer and begin a relationship. Approach him / her on LinkedIn and talk about how good you would be for that position but, not in an off-putting way. On the off chance that this doesn't go well, it is OKAY. At any rate you attempted.

## 5 things should do after the interview meeting

### 1. Proceed with the pursuit of employment

It's not over till it's over. A meeting does not promise you the occupation. You should know that you were met alongside different candidates – presumably in a long line. So until you get that telephone call complimenting you for being chosen for the organization, keep sending those resumes.

### 2. Say bless your heart

You don't lose anything by communicating something specific of appreciation to the organization or the questioner. Simply send a basic card to say thanks for considering your application. Expressing gratitude toward them can extend a picture of an appreciative and mannered candidate and gain you some brownie focuses on your application.

### 3. Assess

Directly after the meeting, review what happened. You have to begin by posing these three key inquiries:

- What turned out badly?
- What went right?
- What can be altered?

### 4. Keep in mind the troublesome inquiries

Observe the inquiries you were asked amid the meeting, particularly the troublesome ones. You may very well experience them again.

*5. Make a subsequent call*

It's never wrong to call and get some information about your status. Simply don't be excessively meddlesome or pushy. Now and then the HR Department acknowledges a call and considers it to be a pointer that you're an extremely motivated candidate. Then again, being excessively constant may give the feeling that you are anxious; this could affect your application in an unpleasing manner. Remember the word 'patience'.

## Meet Thank You Notes

The best meeting cards to say thanks are short, compact and just take a couple of minutes to compose. The principle motivation behind them is to keep your name before the employing powers after your meet-up.

On the off chance that you damage your first-impression, all the meeting cards to say thanks on the planet wouldn't turn things around; be that as it may, in the event that you are one of the main three competitors, it could have any kind of effect regardless of whether you get tapped for the position or not.

Here are some sample formats of a test thank you letter:

**Test Letter 1**

Dear (Manager's name),

Thank you for meeting me on Tuesday for the (name of the position)'s position. I walked out of your office with a sentiment fervor that I am certain I can add to (name of the organization)'s developing achievement.

(List your prominent qualities relevant to the position you applied for.)

I anticipate getting notification from you soon, and welcoming your feedback as well.

Greetings,<br>
(Your name)<br>
(Contact Number)

**Test Letter 2**

Dear Ms. Desai,

Much obliged to you for meeting me on Wednesday for your Business Director Position.

Plainly XYZ Corp is exceptionally specific about who they employ. I respect that in an organization, and can guarantee you that I convey to the table a solid hard working attitude, as well as a predictable reputation of top execution. My references will bear witness to my achievements and authority capacities.

I respect your criticism or inquiries, and anticipate the following stride in your meeting procedure. I'm accessible to meet with you again on Thursday or Friday of one week from now, or Monday or Tuesday of the next week.

Best respects,
Veena Ramchandran


## 10 Key Questions About Interview Thank You Notes...that matter

*Do you really need to design and mail it...or is it OK to send an email?*

Yes, it's OK to send an email nowadays; in any case, sending an email doesn't have a similar effect on individuals. A great many people I know get huge amounts of email each day.

*Be that as it may, how many individual letters wind up around your work area nowadays?*

An email card to say thanks is fine, however for full effect, take the additional time and send a sort kept in touch with one. It's not important to set up a written-by-hand letter.

Your objective all through the meeting procedure is to emerge. In all likelihood you will rival against other candidates...many of whom won't try to compose a letter and will simply shoot an email.

*Who have to get this thank you letter?*

The answer is; everyone who talked with you. Ensure you gather business cards from everybody amid your meeting.

Along these lines you now know the right spelling of their name and title.

*If six individuals talked with me, is it OK to send each of them a similar letter?*

No. The general merriments in the primary section can be the same, yet customize your meeting cards to say thanks by changing 1 or 2 sentences.

*Is there a contrast between meeting cards to say thanks and meeting thank you letters?*

Not generally. Fundamentally, a prospective employee meeting card to say thanks is a short letter.

*What if I'm not certain I truly need this employment? Should the tone of my meeting card to say thanks still be certain and seem like I need the employment?*

When in doubt, seek after the position regardless of the possibility that you are not so much beyond any doubt whether you need it or not. There are several cases of how prejudging an open door could reverse your chances of getting the call.

Recollect that, you are in the driver's seat, not the organization. You can simply turn down an offer. However, in the event that you don't get an offer, you don't have any alternatives.

It's constantly astute to finish the meeting procedure and consider everything you can before settling on your choice.

All things considered, on the off chance you know without question that you don't need the employment, still send a positive thank you letter. Specify that you anticipate hearing once again from them, yet don't recommend you need the employment.

*After I send my meeting thank you letter, on the off chance that I don't hear anything, would it be a good idea for me to call the supervisor for an update?*

Yes. Mail your letter either the day of your meeting or the following day in the event that you set out your meeting.

Seven days after you drop your letter via the post office, call the respective authority.

Attempt to picture what is happening at the flip side of the procedure. It takes two days for your letter to arrive. Your 'meeting thank you' may sit in the director's in-wicker bin for 2-3 days before really being perused.

Thus, 5-6 days have gone since your meeting. This is flawless planning as your letter just reminded them it's a great opportunity to accomplish something.

On the fortunate chance that you did well in your meeting, they won't have any desire of losing you, so they will get the telephone and allow the HR to welcome you back, or possibly begin the offer procedure.

*Should I leave a phone message if the administrator doesn't get the letter?*

Absolutely. Give innovation a chance to work for you. Your central goal is to either keep the enlisting procedure moving, or cut off things so you can move on.

A phone message will clear doubts.

*If I met with 3 or 4 individuals, who do you advise me to call?*

Some of the time the HR Manager will instruct you to just work through the HR division. In the event that you choose to by-pass them and talk specifically with the contracting supervisor, it could irritate a few people.

Having said that, you are constantly happier managing straightforwardly with the chief. Customarily the chief will give you their business card and say, "call me in the event that you have any inquiries".

This is obvious that the director you will answer to, generally is the decision maker. Thus, dependably call the enlisting supervisor first unless coordinated generally.

*What number of circumstances would it be a good idea for me to encourage development if nobody is getting back to me?*

I have a 3-strike rule and you're either out of the show or run the show.

You should set aside the opportunity to meet with them. You sent them a thank you letter. You should have the kindness of opportune input.

On the off chance that you need to continue approaching them, then the answer is that you should stop. It's essential to shut things off in your brain and move on.

On the off chance that you continue thinking about it and reflecting on things over and over in your brain, you'll simply get confused and de-motivated. It makes no sense worrying over it any more if the organization is keeping you out of the loop.

I would say, a large portion of the organizations out there will give you a convenient input. The other half will either abandon you hanging inconclusively, or in the end hit you up at whatever point they get around it.

On the off chance, this is how they treat you on your first date, what will they resemble when you get hitched?

Along these lines, here are the means by which you can get conclusions to this in an expert way, with no feelings overflowing.

Call the procuring administrator 7 date-book days after you send your 'meeting thank you letter'.

On the off chance that you don't get a response (strike one)...call them once more.

On a positive note, if you get a phone message, leave another wonderful message requesting input.

Let an additional 48 hours pass by.

In the event that they don't get back to you (strike two), either email or send them the accompanying message:

Hello there Diana-

This is Peter calling once more. Trust all is well with you.

I haven't got any input from my meeting held 10 days back. I'm detecting now that you've presumably enlisted another person for the position.

On the off chance that I don't hear once more from you before the days are over tomorrow, I'll quite recently accept that you've closed your position. Thank you again to take an ideal opportunity to meeting me. It was a delight meeting you and kindly remember me for any future openings.

STRIKE THREE!

The above message utilizes a capable deal procedure called "a take away". Either of two things will occur now. They will call you in a frenzy and say, hold everything, too bad for the postponement, when would you be able to return for a prospective employee meeting.

On the other hand the quiet will continue...and you realize what that implies.

The main reason for this message is to provoke a procuring power to make a decision...even if it's to let you know, no way. Whatever you do, don't continue calling and calling and calling the director like a stalker competitor. Stay with the three strikes and try to run the show.

In case you're working with an official selection representative, don't just call anyone in the organization. Work through your selection representative.

Yet, in the event that your selection representative is giving you the noiseless treatment, do the three strikes and you're settled.

## Genuine Story

I came across this story online when was researching on the topic. The story is written in the manner narrated by the man, with whom this happened.

As an official selection representative, I was working with an incredibly hopeful candidate. I was extremely inspired with his interpersonal abilities, and our discussions were constantly warm, proficient, and well disposed.

Soon after we began cooperating, he wouldn't get back to me or react to my messages.

In all honesty, I not only discovered that this individual was acting strange, I was also getting angry about it.

I utilized my three strikes but to no avail.

Along these lines, I cut off things in my psyche and proceeded forward.

Around two weeks after the interview I got a calming email from his significant other advising me that Vineet had met with a genuine cruiser mishap.

They anticipated that he would live, however he would confront an extremely extensive recuperation. She expressed gratitude toward me for my email and follow up calls.

Imagine a scenario where I had permitted my feelings to outwit me and had left Vineet an irate phone message berating him for not giving back my calls.

Continuously assume the best about individuals. You're not a mind reader. You never recognize what could happen in somebody's life at any given time.

Despite somebody's conditions, the strike three lead works.

It is an expert, non-enthusiastic approach to reclaim control and to get a conclusion without cutting off any ties. Do try it...on any off-chances!

# CHAPTER 13

# 12 Tips to Perfect Your Job Interview

In this last chapter, I have decided to go simple and give you the last minute tips for success. Keep these tips always in your palm in order to proceed with a smooth and impressive interview.

## Greet the interviewer as Ms. or Mr.

Many people around you prefer that you call them by their first name, however, in the case of your interviewer, neither he is your friend nor your acquaintance, call them with their last name.

You must be thinking, what is the big deal in calling a person with his last name? It is often considered that calling a person with his last name indicates that he is being respected. Calling the interviewer using the first name might not be a big deal for some, but many prefer that they receive respect for their position as an interviewer.

An interviewer judges the interviewee every moment and giving a little bit of respect will not harm your dignity at all. When you call someone with his or her last name, you are basically conveying a message that "I respect you and you are very important".

Also, you can stand out by showing some respect yourself. You never know, this might even be the key to get you hired.

## Mobiles switched off, not on vibration

It is extremely embarrassing when your phone rings during an interview. The expression on interviewer's face may turn red in an instant. Trust me, if your phone rings in an interview, it is the worst call you will ever receive in your lifetime.

*Before you enter the interview room double check that your mobile is switched off. Do not lose a good job opportunity just because of a small avoidable error.*

Make sure phone is switched off and not on vibrate. The worse situation you can have after your phone rings in an interview is to keep it one vibration mode. The bee like sound is much more irritating than the ringtone your phone has.

If your phone rings in an interview, the interviewer may think that accidentally you forgot to shut it down, but if it vibrates, your interviewer may come to a conclusion that the interview is not the most important thing of your life in that situation, Of course it is!

Do not lose a good job opportunity just because of a small avoidable error.

## Maintain the eye contact and smile

I have stressed enough in this entire book about the importance of body language and I don't mind mentioning it again because it is so very important.

I'm sure you must have heard about the phrase, "I didn't trust that man; he didn't look me in the eye."

Looking in the eye creates a very confident personality and it is easy to gain other's trust this way. Looking in the eye is the gateway to looking at your soul. Your eyes project clearly if you are lying or speaking the truth.

I have experienced a lot of students and interviewees in my life who display a very strong personality trait and also many who hide most of the truth and cannot project their true potential.

Eye contact is also very important during a group interview. You have to win the hearts of many instead of one.

Many individuals do not smile when they are stressed. The nervousness can be easily made out because of their tensed facial expression. It's amazing how a simple thing such as smile projects confidence and leadership quality.

However these incidents always taught me how to express my true confidence while speaking to someone important, giving lectures and attending important meetings.

## Handshake Firmly

This is also one of the ways to connect non-verbally. It sounds almost like a joke when people judge others because of their limp handshakes. But it is true and it happens.

A firm handshake symbolizes confidence and a strong character.

Meanwhile, you don't want to be too manly, especially when a man is shaking hands with woman, being too firm might hurt the person.

There is a friend of mine who crushes my bone all the time we meet. He is a very good friend, but I always try to avoid shaking hands with him. I am sure if he would do that in an interview, it will create an impression about him that he is over confident and dominating.

## Let the company lead the interview

Sometimes it happens so that the person interviewing you is a person of few words. Therefore, there are many silent situations in an interview.

Do not be agitated to move things fast just because you can keep on saying. You may start taking some control and this is not a good thing.

I have seen many candidates in my life who just keep on saying things and do not know when to stop. This is one of the most common reasons for them to get rejected.

If there are many periods of silence then just sit there in silence. If you are confident enough to answer any question, then you have nothing to worry about.

*Be careful not to interrupt the interviewer on the last three words*

I have often noticed that people step over my last 2-3 words of the sentence and then continue talking without extending the courtesy of letting me finish my sentence. It is extremely disturbing.

Be careful not to step over the last three words of your interviewer, let him or her complete the entire sentence. Take a pause for a second or two and then respond to the question asked or add to the conversation.

It is a very common mistake and can happen because of the anxiety and nervousness. You may have practiced the question many times and because you know the answer you tend to answer it more confidently, taking a high risk of interrupting his or her sentence.

Make sure you control your anxiety and wait for the entire question to complete.

*Sit straight and slightly lean forward towards the speaker*

While helping countless working professionals, I have experienced that some candidates while attending the interview are too laid back and enjoying. It is important to understand that this kind of attitude is extremely hated by an interviewer.

The Hiring manager expects the candidate to be very energetic and focused. The best way to give the impression that you indeed are a very energetic and focused candidate is to sit straight and simply lean forward towards the interviewer.

This gives the interviewer the idea that you are listening and interested in what is being said and you are ready to present your views on the topic.

Its quiet amazing that a small gesture like this can send an important signal. And that's why I have been stressing on the body language all along.

*Don't forget to take notes during the interview*

Carry a professional looking notepad with you so that you can take down important notes during your interview. Also, the best benefit of having a notepad is that you can write down the points and ask appropriate questions at the right time.

This is a huge advantage if you ask me and it portrays your sincerity towards the job you are applying for.

Also, a notepad can be used as a cheat sheet during an interview, just in case if you want to refresh your memory or you can't remember the most important keyword for the answer. Also, when I say a notepad, it means a professional looking notepad and not the one's which you carry in your secondary school.

Adding to the benefits, you can keep your important documents like certificates and extra copies of your resume in the binder and when asked for any, you can instantly present them with your samples and portfolios.

Another thing to note down here is to avoid using an iPad or any other electronic devices to take notes, unless and until you are applying for a programmer position or a job in IT profession.

**Do not lose hope until the end**

Halfway through the interview you might be thinking, "I blew it" and hoping that you will never get the job and even if you do, you are not willing to work there anymore.

Trust me, gulp it down and finish what you have started to your best ability. Nobody is forcing you to take the job and it is entirely upon you to decline the offer if it seems best for you. But you never know how the job actually might turn out.

*Rahul made a couple of mistakes in the interview and in the last part of the interview he gave up hope. He could have turned it around.* Even if you are losing the interview, do your best to fight and get a chance to prove yourself, if you really want the job. There are many individuals who did this fatal mistake of prejudicing things too early and paid a heavy price.

So, do not step down until and unless you are absolutely sure that the job will not work in your best interest. The factors that you could consider before rejecting the offer are

- Work load
- Payment
- Location
- Benefits
- Holidays

**Your interview isn't over until you leave the building**

I have heard about many hiring managers who look at the candidates from their office windows till they leave the building and disappear into the crowd. People can do all sorts of things once they are out like, spitting, lighting up a cigarette, shouting at the guard, yapping on the phone for 20 minutes and many other things that are not to be seen by the interviewer.

So be professional until you are out of the area and do not just start celebrating as soon as you come out of the office. Many possess the habit of calling their friends as soon as they are free. Whatever important work you have after the interview, make sure you proceed with it after you are out of the sight.

*There was once an unruly man who parked his car. As he was walking towards the entrance, he stopped in front of the mirror wall of the building to do his one final check.*

*He noticed a few pieces of hair out of shape and to fix them this smart interviewee started to spit in his hands and rub them together and then slick back the out of place hair back to post.*

*The mirrored wall he checked himself in was completely transparent from inside and mirrored only from outside. He had a group interview that day with 4-5 executives and obviously all of the candidates were sitting inside the room where he displayed his disgusting approach to fix his hairstyle.*

**Arrive no sooner than 15 minutes to interview**

Obviously, you don't ever want to be late for an interview. However, arriving too early can sometimes be very annoying to the employer. Since you got there an hour early, the interviewer would be under pressure to start the interview soon.

This actually puts the interviewer in a bad mood and also shows how desperate you are for a job. Do not let your interviewer take the best of you or be irritated even before the interview begins.

**Follow up with a thank-you note after the interview**

You have to send a thank-you note after the interview and it is a must. Do not be late in sending a follow up note after interview.

This is one of the most important interview etiquette and the one which is commonly ignored by most of the candidates. Do not miss this opportunity to put the names of the interviewers forward and the opportunity to give them another indication that you are serious about the position.

Follow these 12 tips to have a smooth transition of your interview to your job soon after. Everyone prefers a well-mannered employee who knows his tasks properly.

Take an extra step and work hard because you know being well prepared is a great advantage and increases your chances of getting that dream job. There is no need to leave everything you like and dumbly prepare for the interview. Enjoy your life and work with dedication at the same time. After all you are working hard to make your life a success. All the best!

# Conclusion

In my entire lifetime I have seen children who have spent years studying, but not reaching any possible conclusion for themselves. They try hard, but the results are never in their favour. These kids work hard, but not in the right way. What they need to understand is that they need to put the efforts in the right manner and that is the key to entire success.

I have dedicated my entire life guiding these children, helping them to understand their true potential and set them on the right path. As a well learned human being, I feel that it is an important duty of mine to help people who are facing difficulties in achieving their goals.

One may find appearing and clearing an interview, a very challenging experience. If you see, there are specific steps that one needs to follow. You can plan and prepare yourself for each step and hence increase your chances of success.

Interview is an important road that will lead you straight to success. You may not get the right job at first, but it is important to know the key to clearing any interview. After training and helping more than 250,000 professionals grow and develop in their career, I have put my ideas and methods to help you clear any interview.

This entire book has been a journey that I have covered since I started growing myself and I really wish that people, who are struggling to find the right fit, will definitely receive help from this guide to clear any interview.

All the points and tricks mentioned in the book are well researched and written in the best possible manner that can help the readers understand the concept easily. Also, I have done my level best to make the book interesting and useful for you. I hope you connect and understand well.

www.ingramcontent.com/pod-product-compliance
Lightning Source LLC
Chambersburg PA
CBHW030317160726
47992CB00005B/2046